Unknown Sands

Unknown Sands

Journeys Around the World's Most Isolated Country

To Best wishes,
John Kropf
March 2006

UNKNOWN SANDS

JOHN W. KROPF

Library of Congress Control Number: 2005938772

ISBN 0-9763565-1-1
Printed and bound in the United States of America

Dusty Spark Publishing
15821 FM 529 Suite #181
Houston, TX 77095

www.DustySpark.com
HOUSTON

DUSTY SPARK PUBLISHING

For Eileen and Charlotte

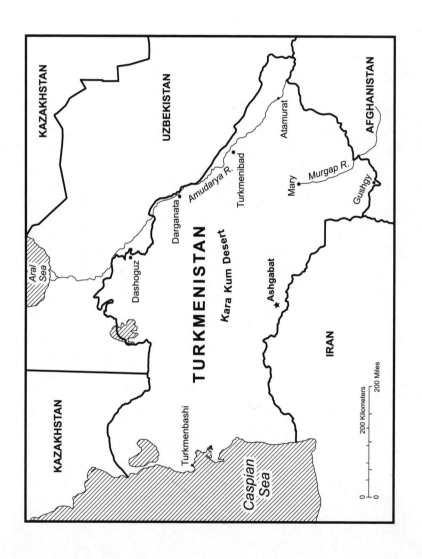

Contents

Author's Note

Central Asia is the kind of place to write mystery novels about…
[Turkmenistan] is a very secretive place.
--Professor Thomas J. Barfield,
The Boston Globe

This book is not intended to be a scholarly work; it is a personal story that blends two years of adventure with Turkmenistan's tumultuous history. My intent is that my experiences and observations will open a small window on its fascinating culture and contribute in some small measure to our understanding of the country. All mistakes are mine alone.

Before moving to Turkmenistan, I discovered little had been written about the country. Other exotic territories like Tibet or Afghanistan have been the subjects of dozens of books in recent years. Strategically located between the hot spots of Afghanistan and Iran, with one of the planet's largest natural gas reserves it remained largely unknown to the West. Central Asia specialists like Fiona Hill of the Brookings Institution have admitted that "we're frustrated by the little dribs and drabs of information that have come in…[h]ow can that be that we have no real clue what's going on there?"

The personal part of this story is one of contrasts between the world of books and reality. Years ago, I started reading Paul Theroux's train travel books and expanded to read everything from Samuel Eliot Morison's biography of Christopher Columbus to Tim Cahill's comic travelogues. In time, I found myself fascinated with the enormous undefined expanse of Central Asia and the accounts of Alexander the Great, Marco Polo, Ibn Battuta, and the later accounts of wayward British Army explorers. Fitzroy Maclean's maverick adventures in Soviet central Asia at the height of Stalin's purges in 1930's were a favorite. Turkmenistan, he said, was a land where Europeans risked "death or slavery." The traveler's tales allowed me to confront the dangers of the Silk Road from the safety of my couch.

In the summer of 2000, I was presented with the opportunity to step outside the world of books and travel to the mysterious places I had only read about. The U.S. Department of State had assigned my wife Eileen to the small American Embassy in Central Asia's most remote and isolated country—Turkmenistan. I withdrew from a secure job and life in the well-ordered suburbs of Washington, D.C. with our two-year old daughter, and followed my wife to what was classified a "hardship post." This was a chance to walk into the same dusty landscape as Alexander and his armies, smell the same dust of the open air bazaars as thousands of Arab merchants had, and eat the same flat bread as Turkic nomads and Buddhist monks had eaten.

In country, I was lucky enough to work for the American Embassy and USAID Central Asia Mission first as a Deputy Country Director then as Country Director. The duties were as completely different from being a Washington-based government lawyer as could be imagined: traveling the country to monitor U.S. taxpayer funded projects in TB hospitals, irrigation projects, clean-up of the Caspian Sea, and attempts to form local civic organizations. While moving around in

Turkmenistan is not impossible, many of its internal state security controls make it difficult (ironic since this had once been nomadic territory). My official status as a member of a diplomatic mission helped in accessing some of the country's restricted zones. I had the opportunity to travel extensively to all five of the country's *welayatlar* (provinces).

Following September 11th and the uncertainties of sharing a 750-mile border with Afghanistan, my wife was authorized to return to the States with our daughter. I expected to follow on in a matter of weeks. There was an immediate demand for sending humanitarian relief to the war and to the famine ravaged Afghanistan people by way of a land route from Turkmenistan. The American Embassy and USAID were critical to that effort and instead of a few weeks, my stay extended to eight months.

Turkmen, Russian and Mongolian names have been transliterated into Latin script with a confusing variety of spellings. I will borrow Stanley Stewart's disclaimer for *In the Empire of Genghis Khan* when he "opted in most cases for a form that is acceptable to modern historians, but in places consistency has been sacrificed to ease. Purists may be appalled by 'Genghis' and 'Kubalai' but general readers will avoid the irritation of familiar names rendered in unfamiliar guises."

As an employee of the U.S. Government then and now, I should also disclaim that views contained in this story are mine alone, and not those of the American Government.

--JWK

Unknown Sands

JOURNEY 1

Death or Slavery?

[Turkmenistan] was more than ever a region, which no European, indeed no foreigner, could visit without risking death or slavery.
--Fitzroy Maclean

For centuries, Turkmenistan was the world's most feared territory. Since the time of the Mongols, the nomadic tribes of its vast desert wastes were deemed ungovernable. Russians and Persians were captured and carried off by the fierce Turkmen to be used or sold as slaves. Europeans avoided traveling through the area at all costs. It was not until the late 19th Century that Turkmenistan—the last of the wild Central Asian territories—was finally subdued by the Russian Army. Now, it is an independent country strategically located between the hot spots of Afghanistan and Iran, and sits atop one of the planet's largest natural gas reserves. Still, Turkmenistan is virtually unknown to the outside world. This was where my wife, two-year-old daughter, and I would live and work for two years that included September 11th, 2001 and a war in next-door Afghanistan.

* * *

"You're moving where? For how long? To do what?" were the first questions from my father.

"Turkmenistan. For two years. Eileen will be the Political and Economic Officer for the American Embassy," I explained, trying to sound as though this was a normal company transfer to a branch office.

The idea only *sounded* illogical and risky I told myself. We would be completely safe moving to Central Asia's most forbidden and isolated country.

There were some complicating factors. I had no experience living overseas. We had a daughter, Charlotte, who had just celebrated her first birthday, and I would be without a job.

"What will you do?"

I could hear the concern in his voice.

"I don't know yet," I replied as if this were also normal.

Days before, the name Turkmenistan had left me stunned as though blinded by a bright flash of light. During our drive home along the George Washington Parkway, in view of the Capitol's monuments, my wife Eileen said the State Department had offered her the assignment at the small American Embassy in Turkmenistan's capital city, Ashgabat.

The Department of State had designated the Embassy a "hardship" assignment. *The Economist* magazine had named it the worst country in the world to live in because of its strict repression of basic civil rights and commerce. Recently, the Turkmen government was forced to deny reports that there had been an outbreak of Plague.

As we cruised the leafy streets of Alexandria, my brain could offer up no point of reference, no mind's eye view of the Turkmen or their land. It was a surprise. The name was only dimly familiar because I had had to memorize it along with the other former Soviet Republics during a college course. It was somewhere "out there." I could conjure up images of Italy, Japan, or Kenya, even if I had never set foot in any of them. They were part of the known world. Turkmenistan was part of the ever-shrinking set of territories considered unknown and mysterious. It was like hearing about one of Joseph Conrad's "blank spaces" on the map that Marlow found particularly inviting in *Heart of Darkness*. The more unknown the better, as if Turkmenistan's obscurity would compensate for the fact that I had never lived overseas.

At home, I opened my outdated *National Geographic Atlas* to find Turkmenistan. The map showed it in the underbelly of the former Soviet Union, intertwined with the four other "stans"—Kazakhstan, Kyrgyzstan, Tajikistan, and Uzbekistan. In 1991 they created a new regional group of Central Asian Republics. Bordered by Afghanistan to the east, Iran to the south, and Kazakhstan and Uzbekistan to the north, Turkmenistan was about the size of Nevada with the population of metropolitan Houston. The cluster of countries resembled a colony of amoebas that were fighting it out to see which one might absorb the others. Turkmenistan stretched out at the bottom of the cluster as though it were a parasite trying to attach itself to the back of Afghanistan. With its small finger of land pointing the way to China, Afghanistan seems poised to use its motility to dart east. Indeed, as soon as the Amudarya River flowed from Afghanistan, Turkmenistan pulled a significant amount of water from the river into the world's longest canal, the Kara Kum. The President of Turkmenistan saw a grander shape—suggesting that his country gave the appearance of a wild bull charging at the Caspian Sea.

The circuitous borders of the five Central Asian Republics defied a geographer's logic. There was not a straight line among them except for the hammerhead end of Uzbekistan's Karakalapakistan province that abuts the underbelly of overlying giant Kazakhstan. As if to make up for this, Uzbekistan's eastern border was a jagged pair of jawbones that looks as though it were about to swallow western Kyrgyzstan and northern Tajikistan.

The impossible jigsaw borders were the design of Joseph Stalin and his Tsarist predecesors in an effort to keep his newly conquered republics mixed with multiple ethnic and tribal groups, thereby preventing any group from mounting a significant force against the empire. The tortured lines defied both natural and tribal boundaries. Where a major river like the Amudarya might serve as a natural border between Turkmenistan and Uzbekistan, the Russian-drawn border zigzags back and forth across the river, sometimes putting the entire water course in Uzbek territory while other sections are entirely under Turkmen control. Travelers on the Amudarya could never be sure which country they were in.

Likewise, the Central Asian national capitals, cities that would normally be somewhat centered in a country, were all oddly situated at the country's margins. The capitals of Tashkent, Ashgabat, Bishkek, and Almaty are all less than 20 miles from a border, with Dushanbe at about twice that distance.

Of the five countries, Turkmenistan was the greatest mystery. Only a handful of intrepid British explorers from the late 19th and the early 20th Century, along with a few curious journalists and carpet fanatics, had trekked there to report on the land and its people.

The country had always been subsumed as part of larger indefinite, geographical regions with names like Khorezm, Tartary, Transoxus, Turkmenia, Transcaspia, and Turkestan. Before its conquest by the Russians in the 1880's, the territory was never considered a country in political terms. Its boundaries were undefined and its people were deemed ungovernable despite repeated attempts to subdue them. While the Turkmen tribes had been the last to submit to Russian rule, it came at a terrible cost. There are some who doubted it should even be a country at all; that it should instead be returned to its natural, pre-Russian existence that was nothing more than harsh desert sparsely occupied by fierce nomadic tribes. The country represented the southernmost reach of the Russian Empire in the Great Game with Britain.

At Turkmenistan's center is the Kara Kum Desert, or Black Sand Desert, which dominates eighty percent of the country. The Kara Kum is not a land of graceful windswept ridges of Arabian gold sand about which T.E. Lawrence might have romanticized—the Desert instilled fear and melancholy in Europeans. In the 1880's while traveling the Trans-Caspian Railroad, a young Lord Curzon pronounced it the "sorriest waste that ever met the human eye." Intrepid British traveler Fitzroy Maclean, a historian of Central Asia and a man used to hardship, described it as a "vast expanse of stony wasteland stretching away as far as the eye could see in every direction varied only by occasional scrub, by low stony ridges or by dunes of soft, shifting sand, shaped by the wind." The only positive account was a 1950's Soviet propaganda publication, which proudly declared that, "every year brings greater prosperity and happiness to Soviet Turkmenia."

After the breakup of the Soviet Union, one of the first travel guides for Central Asia, *Cadogan's*, introduced the country as "only marginally more suited to human habitation than the moon...." Even the more adventurous *Lonely Planet* guide quipped, "it wasn't the end of the earth but it seemed like only a short bus ride away."

Even the origin of the name "Turkman" is complex and indefinite. The term first appeared in the 10th Century writings of the Muslim geographer Maqdisi. One Turkmen tradition traces the predecessor of Turkmen to the Oghuz-Khan, the legendary leader of the Oghuz an ancient Ur-tribe of Central Asia. Maqdisi, used the term "Turkman" to describe the

Oghuz who had converted to Islam. There is an alternate legend that the name is connected to Alexander the Great who borrowed a Persian term to describe Oghuz tribes "as people who resemble Turks." Some have even argued that the term "Turk" is the political term and Oghuz is the ethnic term used to describe the same people.

The first impressions of the Turkmen were as forbidding as the landscape. Fitzroy Maclean described them as "fierce tribes of marauding nomads." Marco Polo had a bad first impression reporting that the "Turkomans...are a rude people and dull of intellect...[t]hey dwell amongst the mountains and in places of difficult access...." His uncles, who had made the Silk Road journey from Venice to Peking once before, had taken the "northern" route through Turkmen territory, stopping in Merv. On their second trip with Marco, they avoided the Turkmen, preferring to go the longer, southern route through Afghanistan. By then, the armies of Ghengis Khan had obliterated many of the Turkmen cities of the northern route. In the following centuries, the Turkmen continued to inspire fear in the European mind. Even after the Russians brutally conquered the Turkmen, journalist William Elroy Curtis, in a trip along the Trans-Caspian Railway, took one look at the Turkmen in their oversized, black shaggy wool headgear and branded them "savage-looking barbarians." Could a people really deserve such a notorious reputation?

As if geographic oblivion, an ethnic identity crisis, and bad travel reviews were not enough, the rulers of this remote territory had long sought to keep the land closed and its people isolated. The close-knit tribal society was highly suspicious of foreigners, preferring instead to kill them or take them as slaves. Indeed, the Turkmen had been feared most for raiding their neighbors of Iran and Russia, it didn't matter which, and selling their populations into slavery. Those who were not captured were killed or deliberately maimed. Travelers avoided it, Maclean wrote, because of the Turkmen's "notorious reputation for cruelty, rapacity and treachery. "

Wary of England's designs on this area and xenophobic, the Russians outright closed Turkmenistan when they took it under control in 1881. American William Elroy Curtis was one of the few outsiders permitted by the Tsar to enter the country in 1911. With his hard-won travel permit he observed: "The regulations are very strict about strangers. The Russian government does not want tourists to come to Turkestan, especially newspapermen, and evidently officials make it as disagreeable as possible for them." Similarly, during the time when Turkmenistan was a Soviet republic, Moscow firmly decreed it to be a closed zone. Maclean attempted to enter several times in the 1930's, only to be arrested by NKVD (the Soviet Secret Police) and forcibly returned to the British Embassy in Moscow.

After independence in 1991, the Turkmen regime, like their tribal predecessors, held an even greater suspicion of foreigners than the Soviets had. Saparamurat Niyazov, who since the Soviet period had been the First Secretary of the Turkmen Communist Party, had become the first president and still remained the supreme decision-maker. He returned the country to a strict Stalinist-style of rule, adopted the title Turkmenbashi (leader of all Turkmen), and bestowed on himself the official title "The Great." Niyazov ordered that a special government committee be formed by the security apparatus to monitor the movement of foreigners and diplomats. Entrance to the country required a letter of invitation approved by the Ministry of Foreign Affairs. Journalists (including representatives of the internationally renowned *National Geographic*) were routinely denied visas. To travel outside the country, Turkmen citizens needed to apply for an exit visa. Even with its independence, Turkmenistan was still considered a closed country.

At the time Eileen received news of her new assignment, the United States was actively working to nudge Turkmenistan away from its own party rule and centrally planned economy to a democratic system with a market-based economy. There was also the issue of its vast energy reserves and how to pay for the vast network of pipelines that would be needed to transport to waiting tankers in the Black Sea or the Mediterranean. President Niyazov wanted the venture paid for by the U.S. taxpayers. The U.S. didn't see it that way. No one could know at the time but September 11th was over a year away and Turkmenistan would prove to be a vital location in fighting the war on terrorism.

* * *

Initial reactions to the news of our assignment from my family and friends were blank stares followed by a short dialogue on Central Asian geography. A few times we had to insist we were not going to Turkey. Explanations quickly turned to subtle discussions about our sanity. Hearing notorious names like "Iran" and "Afghanistan" was enough to change an aunt's quizzical look to unbridled anxiety. Some family members imagined that a seething mob chanting "Death to America" would be waiting to take us hostage at the airport. My mother-in-law's reaction politely summed up our family's thoughts: "Central Asia sounds interesting, but why don't you try for a nice job in Geneva instead?"

Eileen's colleagues affectionately referred to it as one of the "icky-stans." On my way to the State Department Medical Unit to begin several weeks worth of vaccinations for hepatitis A, B, C, D, and E; tuberculosis, rabies, and a rash of other diseases, I met a friend from another government agency who spoke more plainly: "Who'd she piss off to get that assignment?"

When I told friends that we were going to move overseas to a place they had never heard of, I could sense their disappointment. People could understand conventional overseas places like Paris or Rome. Why would anyone willingly give up a comfortable life and move with a young family to the unknown? Even the State Department, which was in the business of staffing embassies worldwide, had such difficulty recruiting its diplomats to serve in this remote region that it offered financial incentives over the regular salary. Questions regarding my sanity were understandable. I had no experience living in a foreign culture, especially one so far removed as Turkmenistan. I was a Government lawyer and had spent my entire career cloistered in Washington's bureaucracy. For eight years, I worked at a desk job giving legal advice as one of over a hundred attorneys in the Legal Adviser's Office at the U.S. Department of State. To an outsider, I was a soldier in an army of federal government bureaucrats working in an agency with its own language of acronyms and impenetrable procedures, ensconced in a large gray concrete building—and I suppose I was. On a typical day at my desk my biggest adventure might be to bookmark the *Code of Federal Regulations* and make lunchtime sojourn to the first floor cafeteria to order Chinese food. There were occasional taxi rides down Constitution Avenue to the United States District Court if one of my cases went to court.

Before Eileen met me, she led a life opposite to mine. Since college, she had lived in England, Egypt, Jordan, and Pakistan; joined the Foreign Service to serve in Dubai (during the Gulf War) and Switzerland; and worked with international peacekeeping forces in the former Yugoslavia. She studied Arabic language and culture, and spoke several other languages as well. A week after we were married she was sent on a trip to Bosnia and Croatia to report on U.S. peacekeeping efforts there.

For now, Eileen worked on a country desk at "Main State." We owned a brick split level house in a Washington suburb of what seemed like a throwback to a neighborhood set for "Leave it to Beaver." We had family visits on holidays; I mowed the lawn, cooked out, lazily read the Sunday papers and welcomed the birth of our daughter. Life took on a familiar rhythm, yet we knew that eventually she would be assigned overseas not knowing where we might go, but I quietly looked forward to the experience the change might bring to my life.

Eileen and I tried to explain that we wanted the assignment. Eileen's interest stemmed from her studies of Islam in graduate school. She had studied Islam up-close in traditional Middle Eastern countries but the question of Islam's status in Central Asia intrigued her. It had spread and thrived there since the 8th Century but had been suppressed by the last 70 years of Soviet rule. Was fundamentalist Islam simmering just below the surface ready to erupt as had happened with Turkmenistan's neighbors Iran and Afghanistan, had it taken some other form, or was it dead? Eileen wanted to learn for herself.

My own interest was purely as a wide-eyed, armchair traveler fascinated by the Silk Road. I had assembled a small library on the topic, with my favorites being the stories by 19th and early 20th Century British explorers who had a desire to sample oblivion. Most books tended to focus on Tibet, western China, or Samarkand. Turkmenistan had been largely neglected, which only added to its aura of intrigue.

Eileen accepted the position and all that remained was for me to step out of a secure job, sell our house, move the family to a new hemisphere, learn a new language, and adapt to an unknown culture that had almost nothing in common with the West. During the forty-four weeks of Eileen's Russian language training (at the time Russian was still the *lingua franca* among the Turkmen elites), we worked our way through the list of changes.

As a spouse, I was eligible to take the eight-week "FAST" course in Russian. I was never proficient with languages, and eight weeks allowed me to master only the Russian Cyrillic alphabet and to concentrate on a few key phrases that I thought would be handy, phrases like, "Please don't shoot me" and "Was that an earthquake?" or, "Where is the American Embassy?"

* * *

At midnight on Charlotte's second birthday, we boarded a Boeing 767 at Dulles Airport bound for Turkmenistan via Frankfurt and Baku. I staggered through the first class and business class sections under the yoke of four pieces of carry-on luggage plus a child's car seat. With my wide load, I raked glancing blows to the head of every upscale passenger in an aisle seat. Eileen and Charlotte were waiting for me in coach.

Three large, dour-looking German men already in their seats gave long, mildly disapproving looks while I struggled to fit Charlotte's car seat into place.

I seated myself across the aisle, still sensing the collective looks of Teutonic disapproval. I wondered if Marco Polo ever traveled with a two-year-old.

In Frankfurt, we had a fifteen-hour layover. Unlike Marco Polo, we had to maneuver through a sprawling line for immigration and customs inspection on the way to our connecting flight. A squat Jordanian woman in a chador and her family of 10 forced her way between us while repeatedly ramming me in the back of the ankles with her fully-laden luggage cart. Despite my best glares and curt tone of "please stop," she only shrugged, smiled, and continued ramming her cart into my tendons as if it would make the entire line move faster. She might have kept up with the assault had we more time together. All the while, Eileen was pulling a suitcase while precariously balancing Charlotte in her stroller to keep her asleep.

Our departure gate for the flight to Ashgabat was itself a lonely outpost at the end of one arm of Frankfurt's massive airport. Other passengers in the departure lounge included a group of Turkish men, an eight-year-old boy with his mother and a four-stringed folk instrument Eileen said was something called either a "saz" or an "ood" and his mother, a couple of Americans in cowboy boots (probably Texas oil men going to Baku), and an Italian tour group of about a dozen. Feeling like other passengers were sizing me up, I tried to present an air of nonchalance—not easy with a stroller and diaper bag.

The Lufthansa Airbus took us to Baku for refueling. Seventy percent of the passengers emptied out. No one got on. Former employees of the Ashgabat Embassy who traveled this route advised that at this point you should look at everyone who was left on the plane because at some point you will come into contact with them in Ashgabat. A cleaning crew of three stout women entered, one with a gold front tooth, and vacuumed around the dozing passengers. An acrid, sulfur smell, like the kind I remembered from driving through industrial sections of Pittsburgh and Cleveland, permeated the cabin from the outside. It was the output of Baku's oil refineries.

The flight from Baku to Ashgabat was only an hour. The featured entertainment was a Disney cartoon short, *Donald Duck, Jr.* dubbed in German. As we flew in the dark skies above the Caspian Sea, I could not imagine anyone was paying attention to the cartoon except out of bemused curiosity. The only person who might have been entertained was our two-year-old asleep on Eileen's lap.

The plane approached the edge of the Kara Kum Desert in cloudless night. Like the blank space on the map, there were no lights below and nothing to see. We had accepted this assignment and now it was about to unfold.

JOURNEY 2

Ashgabat: Welcome to a Closed Land

Ashgabat means place of loveliness.

--Translation

Ashkhabad [a place of] heat, dust and pestilence.
--Kathleen Hopkirk, A Traveler's Companion

I saw him in the early evening of my second day. He drove an aging, gunmetal gray motorcycle with a sidecar past the front gates of the American compound. The driver was my father's age, in his early 70's, with a dark, leathery face that looked as if it had melted and dried. He had a flowing white beard without a mustache, like those grown by Quaker sea captains of the 1800's. Although he wasn't standing on the foredeck of a three-masted whaling schooner, the effect of the wind was the same. The white, almost iridescent whiskers blew over one shoulder as he piloted his rig west toward the ruins of ancient Nisa. In place of a motorcycle helmet, he wore a black heavy wool *tilpek* hat, the traditional tribal headgear worn for centuries and favored by most of the Turkmen men over 40. He sat erect with a look of resolution as if he were riding one of the famous Ahal-Tekke horses at the head of a caravan. Despite his odd appearance to my western eye, the old man on the motorcycle commanded my respect. His demeanor suggested he was a man of tradition and honor. During his lifetime he must have lived through Stalin's purges, WWII, and the 1948 Ashgabat earthquake, one of the world's most deadly. As a boy, he might have heard a grandparent tell stories of the Battle of Geok Tepe, where Russian troops massacred thousands of the Tekke tribe. For me, the old man was the first genuine sign of this unknown country.

* * *

Two days before, in an unplanned act of timetable symmetry, we had stepped from a Lufthansa Airbus into the deep black of an August midnight. Appropriately enough, we entered Turkmenistan in darkness. The arrival of our flight was the only activity at Turkmenbashi International Airport. On the tarmac a man held up a sign with our last name on it. He did not speak and his tawny, impassive face blended with the shadows. I gained the impression that he would not have understood us no matter what language we attempted as he solemnly motioned us to a waiting van.

Our gloomy Turkmen guide led us inside the terminal to a special room reserved for "commercially important people." Under the sterile fluorescent lighting and gaze of uniformed security officials, I began to realize that our arrival here was not part of an ill-conceived dream. We waited an hour to receive our luggage.

"They probably need time to search through all eleven bags," I told Eileen in an attempt to humor her.

We were cleared through customs and immigration with the help of local "expeditors," men hired by the Embassy whose sole purpose was to assist travelers through the gauntlet of numerous border and security officials. Before we could leave the airport our baggage had to be X-rayed. This was only the beginning of government intrusion. Our phones would be tapped and our movements monitored or restricted. We had no assurance of privacy.

The Embassy had arranged for two Toyota pick-up trucks to drive us to its fenced-in compound located in an area at the south end of Ashgabat called Berzingi. It would be our home for the next two years. Inside the compound, the pick-up trucks took us to a row of sand-colored townhouses that had been prefabricated in Finland, transported in sections, and assembled on the compound. They looked as if they had been transplanted from a middle-class suburb in southern California. We stopped in front of the first of these and our expeditors helped unload our bags.

Seventy-two hours of riding on airplanes and camping out in airport lounges had dulled my senses and left me with barely enough energy to walk out on the deck from the upstairs bedroom of our new home. The 3:00 a.m. view was of a grid of lights laid out on the capital before me. A strip of small, luxury hotels across the road from the compound, one with the name "Kopet Dag," looked like what Las Vegas might have had in its infancy. There was another with Chinese characters. All had billboard-sized portraits of the President over their entrances. Two miles to the east, floodlights illuminated a five-sided, white marble pyramid with cascading water that commemorated Turkmenistan's fifth anniversary of independence. Next to it, under construction, was a white "space needle" monument, topped with a gold crescent moon and five stars to commemorate the ninth anniversary of Turkmen independence. Somewhere in the darkness six miles to the west were the ruins of the Nisa, capital of the Parthian kings and city of the Silk Road. I had the feeling of being inside a bubble. I was not seeing the nomadic tents and blue-domed mosques and madrasas that I had expected in my half-formed image of the Silk Road.

* * *

Waking up in an unfamiliar place is like suffering a momentary case of amnesia. It can be terrifying and exciting at the same time. Waking up in a place as unfamiliar as Turkmenistan, my traveler's amnesia was stronger than usual. I stared at Eileen, who was still sleeping, and around the room at our generic bedroom furniture. My daughter was daughter sprawled in her portable crib with "Lamby" and "Foxy," the two stuffed animals we had allowed her to carry on the plane. Where were we, a hotel in Frankfurt? I staggered to the window and raised a corner of the blinds with one hand. The bright morning light showed we were positioned at the top of a long, high slope facing the southern-end of a medium-sized city, which was a mixture of new white marble buildings and dusty brick homes. The climate was like the American southwest: hot and dry. My orientation began to return. It was the middle of August. I remembered a warning from somewhere to stay inside after 10:00 a.m., out of the sun's scorching rays.

I stepped out onto the porch and remembered that we were on the American compound in Turkmenistan. Looming behind us were the beige, barren Kopet Dag Mountains. The light and shadows highlighted different hues of brown that showed off their crags and crevasses. The mountains appeared as the gnarled fists of an old man. On the other side of the ridgeline was Iran, some ten miles away. Full awareness returned. This was our home in Ashgabat.

* * *

Eileen was expected at work the next day. I got up to watch her dig through our baggage and put on a conservative navy dress. The ritual made sense days before when she was leaving our split-level in Northern Virginia; but not in the middle of a desert. I thought she should be putting on some sort of safari-style khakis with a pith helmet or white flowing robes. I lingered around her aimlessly, like a dog following her from room to room until she gave me a kiss and left the house to share a ride with a colleague to the Embassy.

Most of the Americans lived on the housing compound and drove to the Embassy. On the world scale, Embassy Ashgabat was small. Initially opened in a hotel suite soon after Turkmenistan gained its independence, it had moved to its own fenced-in building a few years later. The American staff represented a microcosm of U.S. Government organization that included an Ambassador, a Deputy ("DCM" in bureaucratic jargon), a Political and Economic Section, a Consular Section, and an Administrative Section as well as the Peace Corps, USAID, and a military attaché. Because of Turkmenistan's size, one person often made an entire section, sometimes two.

Eileen was a Political and Economic Officer. Her duties resembled a newspaper reporter following the local city council meetings, as well as those of a messenger, delivering the views of the home office to Ministry Officials. She was to follow human rights issues including freedom of religion. Months before we arrived, the Government had bulldozed a Baptist Church. Her job would be among the most challenging in the Embassy.

For this first morning I was alone with Charlotte, wondering what to do. The townhouse was equipped with government-issue furnishings and appliances. I had no car and no way off the compound. Our Jeep was still sitting somewhere in the Port of Baltimore waiting to be shipped. The only other daytime occupants of the compound were the guards who patrolled the perimeter and the local gardening crew. Sprinklers ran day and night to keep the lawn on the common area from withering into brown stalks. It was as though Charlotte and I were castaways on an island of green grass in the midst of a brown sea.

For a two-year-old, the isolation did not seem to matter.

We had a TV loaned to us by our Embassy sponsors and a movie from the Ambassador. The only local channel run by the Turkmen State Television showed a highly stylized folk group that looked like a cross between *The Letterman* and *Ravi Shankar*. A chorus of men in white short-sleeved shirts and ties played two-stringed dutars (ancestor to the guitar), sitting bolt upright, while one man wailed a ballad in Turkmen. They played at a fast tempo while Charlotte paraded in a wide circle in an impromptu dance.

"Dance, Daddy!" she exhorted.

I followed performing my own impromptu jig, feeling awkward. I hoped that no one from the Embassy would walk by the window or that Eileen would suddenly return home with the Ambassador.

As I danced, I could not forget that I was on an American island, looking down on a Disneyland of white marble government buildings and monuments. I wanted to find a way outside our guarded enclave to see the real Turkmenistan.

* * *

We hired a nanny, Elena. She was an ethnic Russian in her 40's who had been educated in ballet and piano. Her quiet, smiling demeanor gave her a natural rapport with our daughter. The first day Elena arrived, she brought a small stuffed dog for Charlotte; that day, Charlotte learned her first Russian word, *sabaka* (dog).

Elena was part of a steadily dwindling Russian minority that was leaving Turkmenistan. They had lived here since the 1880's as first class citizens. After independence, the Turkmen government had resurrected its version of Turkmen nationalism, and ethnic Russians were finding themselves out of the University, out of hospitals and out of the government. Many had accepted the Russian offers for dual citizenship and carried Russian passports as insurance in case things became too oppressive. With Charlotte in Elena's care, I was able to explore. The most mundane acts became opportunities for adventure.

* * *

Without a map, I walked out of the gates of the compound in search of an Ashgabat City Bus. When the motorized gate clanged shut, the effect was as though I had just been released from prison. At mid-morning, the temperature was already 111°F. The air burned my nostrils, carrying a stinging sensation down to my lungs. The feeling was the obverse of breathing in sub-zero air during the depths of a Northern Ohio winter.

I walked about two miles and past a block of dirt road that ended in desert scrub dubbed "Whiskey Gulch" by Eileen's predecessor. If I was being followed, I did not notice. The dirt road intersected a modern six-lane boulevard. A Mercedes bus appeared like a mirage out of the waves of heat. Since I had no idea where it was going or the fare, I stepped on and held out an array of local currency for the driver. From the wad of folded bills he handed back, I figured I had paid 50 Manat (either a quarter of a cent or a penny, depending on exchange rates). The bus fares were the only thing I had seen a 50 Manat note used for. I had already thrown away a few of them because they were so worn and soiled that they practically disintegrated when handed to me.

The bus was clean, orderly, and filled with schoolchildren coming home from their first day of school. Boys were neatly dressed in black pants and white shirts with ties. A few of them carried two-stringed dutars cloaked in cloth covers. One eight-year-old boy wore a wristwatch with a gold profile of the Turkmen President on its face. Three girls in floor-length, green dresses and white aprons boarded the bus. The young girls all had exceptionally long, braided pigtails topped with close fitting skullcaps ("*baruk*" for girls; "*tayha*" for boys).

On the stretch of road between Berzingi and the center of Ashgabat, there were a dozen construction cranes erecting more high-rise apartment buildings with white marble facades. Many homes, even new ones, were being demolished to make way for wider roads or more high-rise buildings.

* * *

Ashgabat marked a strategic position in Central Asia where the caravan routes of Merv, Khiva, Bohkara, and Samarkand converged before crossing the mountains to either Iran or Afghanistan. The territory had been a part of Alexander the Great's empire in 330 BC and later passed to the Persian speaking Parthians who ruled it from the nearby fortress-city of Nisa. In the 11th Century, the Turkic speaking Sejulks controlled Ashgabat until its destruction by Genghis Khan's army in the 13th Century. Not a person had been left alive. Not a building was left standing. A shallow pile of rubble was all that remained, soon to be covered over by the sands of the Kara Kum Desert. When the Russians colonized Turkmenistan in the 1880's the site was little more than a small settlement of yurts (round felt tents). The Russians built up Ashgabat as a garrison town, a headquarters from which to consolidate their control of the Turkmen. In the 1960's, when the Soviets were excavating for the foundation for a new hotel they found the remains of an ancient city nearly 2,500 years old.

Ashgabat was again undergoing a complete makeover, this time at the personal direction of the President. Whole neighborhoods were being demolished to make way for wide avenues. The *Hakeem* (mayor) of Ashgabat would order bulldozers to demolish homes seemingly with only a few hours notice to the occupants. French and Turkish construction companies were erecting rows of white marble high rises. Like Berlin in the 1930's or Bucharest in the 1990's, dictators remade their capitals by leveling blocks of old buildings to remake grand avenues.

* * *

The closer we got to the city center, the more I noticed the pictures. I gave up noticing after counting the first dozen billboard-sized portraits of the President. There were so many portraits that they looked out at each other from every direction, every angle. On a downtown street corner, four pictures faced each other as if ready for a game of bridge. The different poses and expressions of the portraits portrayed various facets of presidential personality: the avuncular President, the strong military leader, and even the thoughtful leader.

The full-length, super-sized, gold statues of him often included a cape. One estimate put the number of Niyazov statues throughout the country in the thousands. His picture decorated all denominations of the non-convertible currency. His gold profile was ever present on the upper corner of the national television station. The same two or three pictures were on the front page of the country's four-page daily newspaper. There was also merchandizing: Vodka, men's cologne, tea, and wristwatches—all with the Presidential likeness. It was as if the Government feared that if his image was out of anyone's of vision for more than a few minutes, its citizens would somehow forget the identity of their leader. Still, I wondered if multiple images of the president might lead citizens to some confused state of belief, like children seeing too many Santa Claus impersonators at one time.

Cities, districts, and countless schools and hospitals had also been renamed in his honor. One could drive Turkmenbashi Street to Turkmenbashi Airport, fly to Turkmenbashi City, and toast the President with Turkmenbashi Vodka. Months of the year and days of the week were even renamed after the President or his parents.

To distract myself from the presidential images, I made

an unscientific survey of vehicles on the road in a five-minute period: Lada, Lada, Lada, Toyota Prado (4x4, size of a Land Cruiser), Lada, Lada, old Soviet Army truck, Lada, motorcycle with sidecar, bus, Lada, an ancient, unidentified make of tractor, Lada, Mercedes Sedan (black with smoked windows), Lada, Lada, earth-moving equipment. The Ladas were the VW Beatles of the former Soviet Union—a true "people's car" that came in one shade of white. With year-in, year-out consistency in their square body styles, a five-year-old model looked the same as a twenty-five-year-old model except with fewer dents and pockmarks. In an unintentional irony, the senior Government bureaucrats drove big, black, hard-shell Mercedes. The contrast kept me thinking of old westerns with black hats and white hats.

At a stoplight, a group of twelve-year-old schoolgirls in their traditional costumes of long, green dresses pointed at me, waving and giggling from the open windows of their school. The slogan painted over the top of their school became my first Turkmen lesson: "Halk, Watan, Turkmenbashi" ("People, Nation, Head of all Turkmen"). Like the giant portraits, I soon began to notice the phrase almost everywhere in downtown Ashgabat.

* * *

I stepped off the bus at what I guessed to be the city center, which was marked by a three-legged monument and observation tower dedicated to the country's third anniversary. Atop the tower was a gold statue of the President that rotated to face the sun, his arms raised as if he were commanding its very movement. The tower sat at the end of a square that opened out to a wider plaza where the Majlis (equivalent to a parliament) sat on a base of marble steps. In front of the Majlis building, a giant screen TV on a pedestal broadcast Turkmen National Television all the waking hours of the day. It was still showing what seemed like the same music segment of the combined *Ravi Shankar* and *The Letter-man* group that I had danced to days before with Charlotte. The display was the kind of public relations event normally designed to get the public's attention in a busy place like Times Square. Here the effect was disquieting. The giant TV was without an audience except for a lone soldier who idled in front of the Parliament building trying to show that he was standing guard. There was none of the activity that an American might expect around Capitol Hill. White marble buildings and fountains dominated a lifeless, inhuman setting. The scene was symbolic of modern Ashgabat. This was a public place without any public.

On either flank of the Majlis building, the Ministries of Defense and Justice were being constructed. They had already begun to emerge as large, white-marbled buildings with Taj Mahal-like domes of blue. The Ministry of Justice had a statue of the President's mother holding the scales of justice. The prevalence of so many white marble buildings reminded me of a line from an old English poem, "I dreamt I dwelled in marble halls..." Ashgabat was beginning to look like a melding of Imperial Rome and Universal Studios.

I tried to walk in the shade of the trees in my search for signs of street life. While I would not go so far as to agree with the glowing 1950's Soviet account that the "luxuriant trees make the capitol of Turkmenistan extraordinarily charming, in spite of the fact that it is hard to remain long in the almost vertical rays of the Trans-Caspian sun," I agreed that the best thing the Soviets did for Ashgabat was to plant trees. In 1889, when Lord Curzon passed through Ashgabat on his train trip across Central Asia, he admired the city's "broad streets bordered by small canals and plain trees of maple and cypress." Now, under Presidential direction, thousands of saplings were being planted in long rows around Ashgabat's white marble monuments and outlying desert boundaries. The small evergreens seemed out of place and ill-suited against the intense desert sun. The trees were heavily dependent on irrigation and it was a question how long this could be sustained. In the concrete trough gutters that lined the street, I saw the tree's giant seeds that were the same size and color as brilliant green tennis balls except with a bumpy texture.

In the nearby Russian Bazaar I found life. I looked in the faces of the vendors and the women shopping. Some had high cheekbones and appeared Asian. Others had dark skin and hair; some looked more Indo-European, as if Persian; a few had blue eyes. There were no typical-looking Turkmen, but endless variations on a theme of Turkmen features. Persian, Russian, Mongol, and other bloodlines mixed together. Adventure journalist Stephen Graham wrote in 1914 that within 45 minutes of visiting the city he saw it was crowded with "Persians, Russians, Afghans, Tekkes, Bokharans, Khivites, and Turcomans." Turkmenistan had been at a crossroads of the Silk Road bringing together different ethnic groups, and the Turkmen faces showed it.

Central Asia seemed to be like a giant ocean of constantly sloshing nomadic tribes that displaced each other, intermarried, melded together, broke apart, or, in the case of the Mongols, destroyed entire groups. The Silk Road, like a great current, brought these groups into contact. Histories that stretched over thousands of years were a blur to someone from the New World used to grasping history in increments of a few centuries.

The origins of the Turkmen were murky. Like much of Central Asia, they started as a nomadic people with very little recorded about their own history—much of it borrowed from legends. What seemed to be known was that centuries before Christ, an Indo-European people had inhabited what was present-day Turkmenistan and were later dislodged by a nomadic people from the east.

Post-independence, the country's historians were directed by President Niyazov, as the "First Historian," to begin the official written history with his simplified interpretation of Turkmen lineage that the father of all Turkmen tribes, the Oghuz clan, began here with no acknowledgement of what came before. The Oghuz were the common root of all Turkmen tribes and subtribes that now number over 140.

The men I saw at the bazaar were clean-shaven and neatly dressed. Their downtown summer business attire consisted of dark slacks and short-sleeve white shirts. Despite the dusty streets, their shoes were kept well-polished, while my own had long since been frosted with several layers of brown sediment. Some men wore a suit and tie, usually made out of synthetic material. I wondered how they could wear man-made materials in the stifling heat when Turkmenistan was one of the world's leading cotton growers. In the extreme heat, I expected to see several cases of spontaneous combustion.

Since before the Mongol invasion, the Turkmen had clothed themselves in natural fibers, mostly wool from their hearty breed of desert sheep and some cotton. For cotton, the settled Turkmen were able to use a system of irrigation called *kyariz* which was a chain of wells linked by underground canals, and melt-water from the Kopet Dag transported over long distances with minimum evaporation. A single *kyariz* could take a man a lifetime to build. When Soviet-ordered cotton production began on a massive scale, the landscape had been hastily carved up to build massive cannels used to feed the thirsty cotton crop. Over half of the water was lost due to evaporation or seepage in the unlined canals. Ironically, most all of the cotton, which would have been ideal for the lightweight clothes in desert climate, was exported leaving the Turkmen with imported hot synthetics.

The Turkmen women maintained an air of elegance in their long gowns, especially those in velvet with ornately embroidered *yasak* collars. They looked as if they had just stepped out on the street from a secret formal ball. Women wore waist-length hair up on their heads covered by scarves, following the tradition that the sight of a woman's hair is an intimacy reserved only for their husbands in the privacy of the home. Ethnic Russians were distinct from the Turkmen in features and dress. Both men and women wore distinctly stylish Western clothes. In stark contrast to their conservative Turkmen counterparts, some of the Russian women wore tight-fitting skirts and translucent blouses.

In 1889, Lord Curzon found the town "purely a Russian settlement, though the business quarter has attracted a large number of Armenians, Persians, and Jews. City life is avoided by the Turcomans, who prefer the tented liberty of the Steppe." The Russians made the city their own. In 1899, the Russian Governor General treated a group of twenty-five stalwart English tourists on an adventure tour to a lavish banquet and ball. It was out of character for the normally secretive Russians who were playing the Great Game with England for control of Central Asia to show such hospitality to English guests. As Kathleen Hopkirk wrote, their excuse might have been that "being condemned to living in a remote backwater, the arrival of twenty-five congenial foreigners was simply a good excuse to throw a few good parties." The Russians felt they had been consigned to a remote outpost 100 years ago, but the feeling of isolation remained. It seemed unnatural for a city to exist in this stark landscape.

In 1904, Michael Shoemaker, an American traveler, arrived in Ashgabat just after the city had been decimated by an outbreak of cholera. In the face of the epidemic, the Governor General had staged a banquet in honor of the Tzar's birthday. Many at the banquet died of cholera within 24 hours. The disease claimed a substantial number of lives and is still a problem in today's Turkmenistan.

Ashgabat recovered and began to develop a commercial life, with a cinema, cultural theater, two newspapers, traders, workshops and small factories. At the time of my visit, not a single movie theater remained, Russian ballet and opera had been banned by presidential decree, and the four-page State-run daily newspaper that featured the same stock of pictures of President Niyazov served the city's journalistic needs. Throughout the Middle East and South Asia, in cities like Aman, Cairo, Dubai, and Peshawar, there were bustling commercial centers to be found. In Ashgabat there was no commercial hub. The one thriving commercial area was a giant open-air bazaar, "Tolkuchka Bazaar," located north of town. This may have more in keeping with the Turkmen's Turkic-nomadic roots, which often located their trading centers outside the urban areas.

During WWI and the Russian Revolution, Ashgabat fell into a period of chaos and intrigue. A local group formed the Social Revolutionary (SR) with the hope of establishing an independent state. In 1918, the Bolsheviks sent a ruthless party enforcer by the name of Fralov, who led a brief reign of terror on the city. Fralov summarily shot members of the SR and left one of his lieutenants, Poltrorsky, in charge as he traveled west to the Turkmen city of Kizil Arvat. At the same time, a British secret agent, Captain Reginald Teague-Jones, arrived in Ashgabat, disguised as a Persian trader. He helped rally the remaining members of the SR and Turkmen to assassinate Poltrorsky, Fralov, and the other Bolsheviks. Teague-Jones mysteriously disappeared in 1919 and with him any hope of further British support for an independent Turkmenistan. The Bolsheviks retook Ashgabat and brought Turkmenistan into the Soviet fold in 1924. For a time, they attempted to rename the city Poltoratsk to honor the slain Bolshevik comrade, but the name failed to gain acceptance with the local population because of its association with the reign of terror.

Across from one of the official hotels I found a café that catered to the very few Westerners that manage to find their way inside the country. This was Turkmenistan's only Internet café. Inside, five young Turkmen men were gathered around one of the two computers trying to get a DVD player working. Connecting to the outside world through the country's state-run Turkmen Telecom were next to impossible. After several attempts to connect, the computer dial-up returned what sounded like: the dynamo room at Hoover Damn, a low frequency deep space transmission, and a sack full of hammers in a clothes drier. Even if I had connected, Turkmen Telecom was notoriously slow and openly invasive about reading e-mail.

"Internet ne robotet" (not working), one of the young men said after he saw my frustration.

By this time the group got their PC to play a pirated copy of a Russian dubbed DVD of the latest *Star Wars* movie. One young man wearing a white shirt and a tie with a black vinyl English-style "mac" saw me watching over his shoulder and gave me a thumbs-up. What else could I do but sign back thumbs-up, sharing the success of their newfound entertainment.

* * *

On the late-afternoon trip home, I boarded a bus occupied by women in long traditional dresses and headscarves in the front half and a couple of men at the back. I wondered whether I would have a job or spend my days touring Ashgabat. A sound system piped a bouncy, 1950's "Muzak" version of "Red Roses for a Blue Lady," complete with a full chorus of cheerful white-bread voices singing in English. If the song cheered any of the Turkmen women, none of them let it show. Ashgabat's first impression was as a city of odd-ball incongruities.

I took a seat in the back near two men wearing small, weathered *tilpeks*. One of them carried a ravaged and beaten vinyl bag that looked ready to disintegrate in his hands. His face seemed to match his bag but looked darker and craggier than that of the most weathered Arizona cowboy. Like so many other Turkmen, it was difficult to estimate his age. He could have been anywhere between 45 and 65.

We passed a modern clamshell stadium under construction—large enough to host a new NFL franchise, this will be the third one in Ashgabat. None of them seemed to be used for sports—mostly for elaborate pageants celebrating Turkmen independence and national holidays.

Along the streets, gangs of cleaning crews swept with branches and scooped up road debris in shovels. The only women who covered themselves in this Muslim country were those on the cleaning crews. They shielded their faces from the blowing dust on the roads by wrapping their headscarves around their faces. The wind had picked up to a steady 20 mph, and we passed one of the last sweepers, an old woman steadfastly swiping the street with her branch. The scene illustrated the definition of futility.

As the bus continued in the direction of Iran instead of turning back, I got off at the next stop and walked the last mile home. The road continued in the direction of the Kopet Dag and the Iranian holy city of Meshed. Only 25 years ago, Americans had been on the Iranian side of the border trying to observe what was happening in the Soviet Union. The twist of history was that Iran was now off limits to American officials, but we were now on the Turkmen side, formerly Soviet territory, wondering what was happening in Iran.

During WWII, this stretch of road was used by the Soviets to transport small groups of interned American flight
crews and secretly pass the men across the border into Iran.
The crews had flown bombing missions over Japan and been
forced to land in eastern Siberia. Even though we were allied
with Russia against Germany, the Soviets interned the crews
out of fear that they might incite an attack from Japan. The
Americans had slowly been moved through Central Asia to
Ashgabat where they eventually were allowed to slip out of
the country by pre-arranged "smugglers." In his book *Home
from Siberia*, Otis Hays, Jr. told the story of how the Americans had been received by the British Consul in Meshed and
had been sworn to the strictest lifelong secrecy concerning
their ordeal.

As I walked up to the gates of the American compound, I
looked up at the Kopet Dag to gauge the mountain's mood.
The evening shadows now made them look as though they
were the giant, flexing paws of a mountain lion. The mountains dominated Ashgabat. Not only did the Kopet Dag
mark a political boundary, but it was also a dividing line between Turkic and Iranian civilizations, and even a boundary
between tectonic zones. Ancient cultures both worshipped
and feared mountains. Daniel Boorstein observed that an-
cients also made attempts to imitate them by building zig-
gurats and minarets. I understood this fear and fascination.
The Kopet Dag would change personality depending on the
hour of the day. Sometimes they reminded me of protec-
tive sentinels looking down on the compound, while at other
times they seemed like terrifyingly huge waves that had petrified moments before washing over our outpost and the rest
of Ashgabat. With the final light, they faded into a grayish
purple and then into the black of the night sky. Even at night
I could sense their presence.

* * *

While we slept, the wind blew against the compound with a fierce, erratic energy. It woke Eileen and me at about 3:00 a.m. Charlotte slept soundly in her crib. The gusts reached such a crescendo that I found myself holding stock-still, waiting to see if the roof was going to be ripped off.

"This must be like what the surface of Venus is like," I said. "Or one of those hot-winded planets from a science fiction novel."

"What's that smell?" Eileen said.

Eileen sent me downstairs to investigate the source of the earthy smell. One of our living room windows had blown open a crack; enough to coat the furniture and carpet with a fine layer of desert dust with the consistency of silt. Even after repeated dustings and vaccumings, the smell stayed with us for as long as we lived there. Turkmenistan had made its strongest impression on us by smell.

This was the seasonal "Afghan wind" that could blow for days in late summer.

* * *

When we were able to borrow a car from an Embassy colleague, I drove Eileen to work so I could keep the car and explore farther on my own. We entered Ashgabat's morning rush hour. It felt discordant to behave as if I were driving my old commute in Washington, D.C.

"Sweetie, see if you can find some sort of morning radio show?" I asked out of instinct as if trying to recreate our commute.

"When we find something, do you think you'll understand it?" she asked, knowing my Russian had been only the most rudimentary and my Turkmen non-existent.

She found some static with a twangy, stringed instrument barely perceptible in the background. I waited a bit, hoping the song might end, and we would get a traffic update or weather report. Finally, I could not wait for the end of the music.

"OK, turn it off," I conceded. "Better not to have the distraction."

Traffic laws appeared to be optional, and I needed a calm disposition to concentrate on the traffic. Despite the white lines marking lanes, any space between cars became another lane. The accepted practice for merging was like a game of chicken. Cars filled in blind spots, usually inches off the back quarter bumper.

Lining up at a stoplight was like the start of a sailboat race—cars maneuvered into every gap, practically touching, seeking any advantage at the starting line. There was a yellow light before the green, like at the start of a drag race. It was customary to honk horns even before the green light. With the green light, cars surged ahead. Some were forced to the curb to wait to move back into traffic.

After the third stoplight, Eileen said, "Maybe this is how you drive in a camel race."

"Nomads with cars," I added and then tightened my grip on the steering wheel.

Beyond the normal challenges of post-camel Turkmen traffic, modern Turkmen wedding parties had also adopted the car in place of the camel or the horse. Tradition was that the bride would be wrapped from head-to-toe in gowns and jewelry, carried off in a cart, driven by a male in the bride's family, and the bridegroom would give chase. The cart gave way to the car. Now, nearly everyday, wedding caravans of cars sounding their horns careened down the road in wild processions past the compound, as if they were still in the desert racing on camels.

On Ashgabat's side roads, drivers had to pick their way carefully around ruts, broken pavement, and potholes. Even the sturdiest vehicle risked cracking a strut or shearing off an oil pan. Some manhole covers were missing, creating a hazard for cars and even worse for the unsuspecting pedestrian crossing the road.

More terrifying than the drivers were the pedestrians. Everyone, from a four-year-old child with no parent in sight to the oldest grandmother, seemed to lack the fundamental instinct to fear moving cars. They waded into traffic with a studied casualness. As I sped along with a pack of cars on the busiest of streets, desperately trying to hold my own, clusters of pedestrians moved across the street at a pace timed to meet my grillwork dead center. Instead, they would stop at the white centerline dividing four lanes of traffic. I was not allowed the slightest margin for error; their faces clearing my window by inches. Some were so close that I expected to feel their toes under the tires. Traffic police in gray uniforms walked or stood in the center of traffic with as much confidence as if they had an invisible force field to protect them. The larger bunches of people looked like remaindered formations of bowling pins. I tried not to act on the metaphor.

Driving at night was worse. The entire right lane of a busy street was often filled with people wearing dark clothes as they walked or attempted to hail rides. Local drivers had an aversion to using headlights but still avoided hitting pedestrians—they apparently had developed an ability to sense people in the dark.

Nearing the Embassy, we turned down Pushkin Street, one of the few landmarks that had yet to be renamed in the rush to honor President Niyazov and his family. The street passed a park that held a bust of Pushkin on a pedestal. The bust, once proudly erected during Russian times, now almost seemed to be hiding behind some leafy trees. Across the street was the only other statue of a Russian left in the city: Lenin. He was frozen in mid-gesticulation, pointing an accusing finger in the direction of Pushkin. The Shakespeare of Russia gazed out from his vantage point, his influence no longer a factor. The two Russians were locked in a Turkmen world, their politics, culture, and comrades having abandoned them. Had they possessed the power of thought, they would have known their days were numbered. It was only a matter of time before the Russian statues would be removed, and the street renamed in honor of President Niyazov.

"Try not to kill more than a dozen pedestrians on the way home," Eileen joked, as I let her out at the front gates of the Embassy.

* * *

I was not ready to return to the traffic melee and instead found myself sitting in one of Ashgabat's few outdoor cafes, looking into the impassive ice-blue eyes of a young waitress. With her fair complexion and mini-skirt, she was clearly an ethnic Russian. I had come to the café to try my infantile Russian language ability on a live subject.

"She *has* to talk to me," I thought.

Studying the menu, there was a long list of cigarettes for sale just after the desserts section. It was clear that western tobacco companies had been one of the few to make inroads here, especially Philip Morris. There was a "Marlboro Kafe" listed on my homemade map of Ashgabat, but it seemed the other four or five cafes in town also qualified. They shared a décor of "Marlboro" umbrellas, menu boards, ashtrays, ashtray stands, and the distinctive red, black and white outlines of the familiar logo.

I imagined mastering enough Russian to say to the waitress, "I'll have the eggplant, *shashliek*, and a carton of Marlboros for dessert." Instead what I think I said was, "I am thinking good. May I want coffee?" She did not suffer my attempts at Russian gladly. Without a smile, she turned and walked off, leaving me to guess whether I had made myself understood or insulted her.

I regretted now that I did not discipline myself to study the language. Merchants like Marco Polo grasped new languages out of necessity. Languages traveled freely with the commodities of the Silk Road. One of my Turkmen friends, fluent in Turkmen, English, Russian, German and some French, later told me that a man with one language has one life, but a man with two languages has two lives. I compared it to being adrift at sea. Without language, I had little to hold on to. After the cold stares of the waitress, I felt I as if I were clinging to a deflating life raft looking for an island. With more ability, I would have had a small island to which to cling for safety. More ability still, and the island would grow until it became a landmass big enough for a whole country, allowing complete freedom of movement.

Even if I had been able to order in perfect Russian, the waitress and I would have been speaking in a language that was now officially shunned. While Russian was still spoken in everyday life, especially in the cities, the President had decreed that Turkmen would be the country's official language. The decree was accompanied by an insistence of racial purity of senior state officials. Overnight, teachers, doctors, government workers, and students had lost their jobs because they did not know the Turkmen language. Our nanny, Elena, had been a civil engineer during the days of the Soviet Union.

The difficulty even for Turkmen was that under Soviet rule the official language taught in the schools and used by government had been Russian. To keep their jobs, many of them had to learn their ethnic language overnight. The Turkmen language itself had a tortured history. It had originally been recorded in Arabic script, but then under the Russians had been changed to the Cyrillic alphabet. Now the Government was transferring Turkmen to a Latin alphabet in an attempt to connect with the Turkish language.

The waitress returned to my table with a "shepherd's salad" of chopped tomatoes and cucumbers and watery instant coffee. Even without adapting to the language, I at least noticed a small change in my attitude about food hygiene. I no longer minded flies on my food; I just didn't want to see them on it. This would eventually change to "I do not mind flies on my food even when I see them."

Drinking bad instant coffee, I wondered what chances I had of learning about the Silk Road if I could not even order lunch.

* * *

During our first weeks, we slowly made friends, but no Turkmen were among them. One night, our family went to dinner at the home of an Embassy colleague. Located behind a wall on a small, unnamed alley, the neighborhood was shabby in a misleading sort of way. Small gangs of boys played in the street, while some rolled an old bicycle tire down the sidewalk, trying to guide it with a stick, like a scene out of 1890's America. After we made a wrong turn, a group of about a dozen kids surrounded our car. We stopped at a construction trench that broke deep into the surface of the road. The small gang was yelling at us, and I could not tell if it was meant as a warning not to cross, or to encourage us to attempt the trench, get stuck, and provide entertainment. We crossed successfully and, regardless of their intentions, they cheered our success.

The house was what a mid-level, Middle East potentate would have lived in. We stepped through a door into a courtyard sheltered with trellises of grapevines and small, twisted mulberry trees. Two kittens played among the flowerbeds. From the courtyard, we moved into a dining room and then entered a large sitting room through heavy, lacquered wooden doors. A 12-year-old Turkmen girl served as baby-sitter for our daughter and the child of another couple. Eileen and I were offered gin and tonics from a fully-stocked bar.

Our host was telling a story about two Ambassadors at a diplomatic function debating the translation of the name "Ashgabat."

"The first ambassador claimed it meant 'the place of passion'" offered our host to the small collection of guests. "But the second ambassador disagreed, saying it meant 'place of tears.' The two went back and forth like this for some time. Then, the French Ambassador casually dismissed the entire controversy by offering a back-handed compromise."

Our host paused to for a moment, almost as if he was offering a punch line to a joke and then said in a bad imitation of a French accent, "Passion...tears...zey are really one and the same, eh?"

The electricity went out seconds after he ended the story. A generator on premises quickly revived it. During the four-course dinner, the lights continued to flicker.

Coffee and cognac were served in the courtyard that was now layered with handmade Turkmen carpets for sale by two local women. Drinking coffee and watching the carpet sellers throw out their hand-woven tribal rugs left me with the feeling that I had stepped into something like the poor man's Raj.

We drove home that night past the white marble government buildings when I said to Eileen, "This feels like a bubble, like we're separated from the real Turkmenistan."

"It will help when you get a job," she said. "But I know what you mean. I'm inside the Embassy most of the day. It's a windowless office. I need to get out more."

We lived in a fenced-in world, and she worked in windowless one.

I thought again of *Heart of Darkness* with Conrad's description of sailors who touched distant ports. Their casual excursions in port were enough. For some Embassy colleagues the same was true for Ashgabat. Working in the Embassy, living on the compound, and eating at the few restaurants that catered to the handful of western diplomats would get them through two years. I was anxious to leave the city. Out there was the secret of a whole country and its forgotten connection to the Silk Road.

* * *

Some nights later, I was dozing on our couch and wondering if I might be hired by the Embassy to sort mail when I felt a side-to-side motion for about ten or twelve seconds. I got up and saw the light fixture over the dining room table gently swaying, which confirmed I wasn't imagining things.

I called up the stairs to Eileen, "Sweetie, I want you to come downstairs and bring Charlotte."

Eileen came down holding Charlotte who was holding Lamby.

"What's wrong?" she said.

"I think we experienced our first earthquake," I said.

We paced around for about 30 minutes. Charlotte seemed generally puzzled by our state of anxiousness. Eileen and I discussed the need to "do something" like go outside. We slept on the second floor thinking we would have a better chance of being rescued from the debris if our prefabricated townhouse collapsed.

The next day, the BBC news service confirmed that an earthquake centered about 40 miles away in Northern Iran had registered 3.0 on the Richter scale. Turkmenistan's media said nothing about the tremors. The President had declared the "Golden Age" (Altyn Asyr") of Turkmenistan and nothing, not even nature, could change the constant reporting of only positive developments.

Ashgabat was in a powerful seismic zone. At about one in the morning of October 6, 1948, an earthquake had leveled most of the houses and buildings in the city, killing over 110,000 people—over two-thirds of the population. Measuring 9.0 on the Richter scale, the destruction was so complete that only a Russian-era bank was left standing. Nearly everyone who has lived in the city has a family story about the devastation of that quake through a parent or grandparent. Initially, the Soviet media denied the reports, but later admitted the disaster. The President was orphaned when his mother was killed. The date is still marked as a national day of remembrance in Turkmenistan.

A month after our first earthquake, a more powerful one struck in eastern Turkmenistan, killing several dozen people. Neither the deaths nor the earthquake were ever reported by the government media. Like the old Soviet controlled media, the Turkmen media believed that if the earthquakes were not reported, they did not exist.

* * *

By the end of the first month, I was hired to work with the small development program for USAID. Larry, the sole American who had been running the program in Ashgabat, had 20 years experience in development, mostly in Africa and a few years in the Middle East. He carried a distinct west-Kansas accent and dressed in cowboy boots and vests and had grown up around horses. Twice a week, he rode the local Ahal Tekke horses at a stable located at the mouth of the Firuza Gorge. One hundred years ago, he might have been riding the Chisholm Trail as a cowboy.

The job required travel to remote corners of Turkmenistan inspecting the small group of U.S.-funded projects. My biggest challenge, however, continued to be language. The first day, I was trying to heat up some coffee in the Russian-made microwave when a little bell chimed and a female voice exclaimed in Russian, "Dver Atkri!" An appliance was talking to me and I was struck dumb with my inability to comprehend. I assessed likely interpretations: warning lethal radiation, the Russian Army is coming, or open the door. I opened the door and took my coffee.

The dangers were even greater when the day before I tried to negotiate my first haircut with a large ethnic Russian woman. The dialogue consisted of the following:

Me: "Nimnoga, Nimnoga!" [a little, a little!]

Haircutter: "[a staccato stream of Russian, which I translate as "I'm giving you a green Mohawk whether you like it or not.]"

Me: "Ooo Menya Yest Cowlick." Pointing and hand gestures. [I have a cowlick.]

Haircutter: [Quizzical smile, more Russian.]

I came out severely shaved at the back of the head but was otherwise unscathed.

How could I travel to the four corners of Turkmenistan when I could not understand my microwave or get a haircut?

* * *

The second day on the job, Larry asked me to visit a polytechnic institution at the edge of town to learn about its fledgling program to develop a cadre of entrepreneurs by teaching basic business practices. With a driver and an interpreter, we pulled into a deserted parking lot across from a wide square of concrete buildings baking in the sun. The building paint was chipped and peeling. Cracks ran along the concrete block walls. Weeds pushed up through breaks in the sidewalk. It looked as though Soviet Army cadets might have once used it as a setting to conduct military exercises in urban warfare.

Inside, an instructor and her assistant awaited us on the second floor. We were treated to green tea and biscuit cookies as they described their curriculum, which was based on the practices of the American youth organization Junior Achievement. They were clearly dedicated to teaching principles of entrepreneurship—in a country that did not want anything to do with free enterprise. The government wanted only to control in the way of the old Soviet-style command economy. Small businesses would start up and suddenly be closed down. Internet access had recently become available in Ashgabat, but the Government had now closed Turkmenistan's only two Internet cafes. Those Turkmen lucky enough to have independent access to the Internet had all their e-mail monitored by the country's sole Internet provider, Turkmen State Telecom.

As I sat through the presentation, I was preoccupied with the thought that only 120 years ago, the ancestors of my hosts had been the last of the wild Central Asian tribes to be subdued. For centuries, since the collapse of the Empire of Ghengis Khan, the Tekke Turkmen, the fiercest of all the Turkmen tribes, had been feared. The Tekke were the last of the Central Asian tribes to submit to Imperial Russia. They extended their independence by humiliating the Tsar's army in a disastrous defeat in 1879. This act advanced their long-standing reputation as ungovernable and, as Maclean said, "fierce nomads with lasting allegiance to none."

Russia had sent a reprisal force in 1881 to crush the Turkmen at the battle of Geok Tepe. They laid siege to the giant mud-walled fortress of the same name and mortally breached one wall with mines and artillery. The Russian cavalry slaughtered twenty thousand Turkmen, mostly women and children. The Russian General Skobelev took no pity on them, believing the magnitude of the massacre proportional to the length of peace. Later that year, at the Merv Oasis, the final stronghold of the Tekkes, the last of the Turkmen surrendered without a fight.

Since then, the Turkmen had been "civilized" and lost all signs of their wild independence. It was a remarkable change. The group of 25 English tourists that the Russians entertained in 1899 were treated to a mock battle between Cossacks and Turkmen militia featuring a double cavalry charge. In a few short years, the ungovernable Turkmen seemed to have undergone a complete change in character, becoming like the Native Americans who performed in *Buffalo Bill's Wild West Show*. Lord Curzon was convinced that the Turkmen had been completely cowed when he saw a number of them in the service of Russia wearing uniforms of the Tzar's Army. "The spectacle of these men," observed Curzon, "only eight years ago the bitter and determined enemies of Russia on the battlefield, but now wearing her uniform, standing high in her service and crossing to Europe to salute their sovereign the Great White Tzar."

The modern populace appeared docile and compliant. No matter what hardship—destruction of their homes, loss of businesses, erosion of their children's education—they show no hint of their once ungovernable disposition. In the 1920's, Moscow seized and divided tribal lands and forcibly collectivized the tribes—all without protest. The minority who objected fled to Afghanistan. Now, even when their family homes were being bulldozed to make way for monuments, fountains, and wide avenues of the new Capital of Ashgabat, they quietly accept the changes forced upon them. What had happened in the last 120 years to make so complete a change in the national character of the Turkmen from the most feared to the most docile? During my two years, it was one of the greatest mysteries to me. Were they so fully dominated and beaten down by the Tsar and then the Soviets that they had failed to recover their fierceness? Had the magnitude of General Skobelev's massacre been so complete as to drain an entire populace of its untamable spirit?

What had happened to the grand cities like Merv and the people who had developed its flourishing culture? In my first month in Ashgabat, the real Turkmenistan had been kept at an arm's length, just over the horizon, as though I were a foreigner who had come to America and been confined to Disneyland.

As we left the Polytechnic Institution, I was glad to be employed, but I knew my main interest still lay in looking for signs of the real Turkmenistan people, and its place on the Silk Road. I had two years to explore outside the bubble.

JOURNEY 3

Red Carpets in the Bazaar

The best and handsomest carpets are wrought here...
--Marco Polo

I saw my first Turkmen camel suspended against a blue morning sky by a yellow Komatsu crane. His proud new owner had arranged to have the braying beast lowered into a giant Soviet-made dump truck. The transaction was another cash-and-carry sale completed at Tolkuchka Bazaar—the largest open-air market in Central Asia. If Marco Polo were alive today, this is where he would come to replenish his caravan. I had come to Tolkuchka to learn how to shop in Turkmenistan.

For centuries, the bazaars of the Middle East and the Silk Road were focal points for society to gather, learn the latest news, and engage in commerce with locals and foreigners. Nomads had meat and wool. Settled village dwellers had vegetables, fabric, and tools. The bazaars were where the two groups met to bargain for what the other had and what they needed. Sociologists would call it symbiotic. Economists would call it free-market capitalism.

Tolkuchka was part of that long bazaar tradition, dating back to ancient times, but from the Silk Road with its own Turkmen flavor. For Turkmen, it was known as Jygyldyk. A Turkmen friend told me with a smile that it means "a place with lots of sand." It started out as a livestock, textile, and clothing market sometime during the Soviet era (none of my Turkmen friends were sure exactly when) and now it has pretty much everything you can name. It was their giant, national shopping mall where everyone congregated to conduct a lively brand of commerce.

Tolkuchka, the Russian nickname for "push market," earned its name for the aggressive, chaotic nature of the shoppers who must compete in an every-man-for-himself rugby scrum to move among its crowded stalls. Three days a week, individual entrepreneurs from all over Turkmenistan gathered at the site to sell camels, motorcycle sidecars, Iranian-made children's clothes, Pakistani sewing machines, Russian candy and tribal yurt bands. The quality of the goods could vary from flimsy Chinese-made plastic toys that broke on the first day to exquisite hand-knotted tribal rugs that would last generations. There were smaller bazaars in the provincial towns, but none of them could compete with the throng of activity that is Tolkuchka.

* * *

At seven-thirty on a Sunday morning, Enrique, the Peace Corps medical officer, and his wife, Helen, picked Eileen and me up in a white Toyota Land Cruiser. The vehicle was outfitted with a "safari snorkel" that helped the engine breathe through the choking dust of a sandstorm or fording deep river crossings. The contraption looked like a black stovepipe running from the engine compartment to just above the roof.

"Better to get there before the sun burns you to a crisp," Enrique advised as we pulled away from the compound.

North of town, he effortlessly merged into a traffic circle and followed the road over the Kara Kum Canal and into a four-lane melee of traffic that had effectively turned a two-way road into a one-way road.

"Everyone is headed to the bazaar." Helen said. "Sunday is the biggest of the three market days at Tolkuchka Market."

Approaching the bazaar, the road looked like the aftermath of the siege of Stalingrad. The landscape was littered with cracked slabs of concrete and rusting hulks of unidentifiable heavy industrial equipment mired in pools of mud and dust. The parking lot was endlessly assaulted by wave after wave of customers arriving in motley armadas of battered buses, Ladas belching smoke, and boys on camels. The buses were not the brand new Mercedes makes seen around Ashgabat but bulbous, Soviet-era buses coming with families from the countryside. Top-heavy, often listing hard to one side, their bodies were completely pockmarked and dented. The doors to the rear engine compartment swung freely, intentionally left ajar to help cool the engines. The windows of one bus were covered with dingy yellow curtains. They looked as though they were fresh from running a gauntlet of several well-fortified Taliban ambushes.

Three or four men, some with the pretense of uniform (a green smock-style shirt) indiscriminately stopped cars to charge a parking fee of 1,000 Manat (about a nickel) to park in a swath of desert filled with ruts. Their approach was casual not systematic; not every car was charged. It was clear they were not in control of the chaos or even using the money to improve the parking lot. My first instinct was that we protest the fee, but after thinking that these men had the audacity to charge for something so poorly maintained, I decided that they should be rewarded for their ingenuity. Enrique paid the 1,000 Manat.

Parking next to a line of buses, we walked through the

parking lot, and past the motor vehicle section of the bazaar, with over a hundred vehicles parked tightly together. Young men in sunglasses flocked around the cars, from boxy Ladas to nearly new Mercedes and BMWs. The upscale cars had come as gray market imports from Dubai or Eastern Europe. There was even an area for delivery trucks, dump trucks, buses, and earth-moving equipment. My favorite was the motorcycle area with its collection of sidecars. An Embassy colleague was so intrigued by the sidecars that she eventually bought a black motorcycle with a sidecar even though she could not drive it. The rig sat parked in front of her house on the compound.

Outside its walls, the bazaar was ringed by vendors who either could not find room inside or had wares too sizable to be at a stall. Weather-beaten men who squatted before offerings of old machine parts, scraps of wiring and used sections of plumbing spread on tattered canvas dropcloths looked like archeologists displaying valuable finds from a dig. Other groups of men oversaw gaudy furniture, plumbing fixtures, doors, window frames—some salvaged, some new. There was enough material to build and outfit a house. I photographed the world's ugliest couch. Its jagged lines of fluorescent pink and light blue, set against a black velvet background, were reminiscent of a massive coronary on an EKG.

To the west was the livestock section with a menagerie of chickens, sheep, camels, cows, goats, and dogs. This was where I saw the flying camel. Livestock trailers were not available so resourceful farmers used dump trucks to transport their large animals. The creatures had to be loaded into the trucks by crane. Every Turkmen family outside Ashgabat seemed to have room for at least one camel or cow in their back yards.

As I watched the camel transaction, a young man wearing

a *tilpek* walked past us in the direction of the parking lot pulling a flatbed cart with what looked like a matted old coat. I looked closer, it was a black sheep lying on its side with bound feet. She looked resigned to accept whatever fate awaited her. The livestock area was a collection of trucks and makeshift wire pens. A small group of farmers stood and evaluated a cluster of tri-color goats tethered to a post. The other side of the post was a small wire mesh cage, which contained black hens pecking at whatever they could find on their patch of scrub desert. A father and son peered into the back of an old military truck that held a cow the color of red clay. At the far end of the livestock section, men with meat axes stood prepared to butcher while customers waited.

"We can buy camels later," Enrique joked as he reoriented me toward the entrance of the bazaar. He turned me around near a woman selling Turkmen Alabai puppies. Prized by Turkmen tribes for centuries, the dogs would grow to be the size of a Holstein calf and were used to herd and protect their flocks of sheep. Some Turkmen severely cropped the ears of those destined for dog fighting.

We walked up a short dirt incline to Tolkuchka's inner boundary that was partially defined by an eight-foot wall of dusty, yellow bricks commonly used for houses and buildings all over the country. The entrance was a gated portal that led to an uncovered sea of stalls covering some fifty acres. With the mass of people and small front gate, the effect was like pouring a bucket of ants into a funnel. There was enough chaos at the gates to make me think of Dante's entrance to the inferno, "abandon all hope ye who enter...." Eileen and I squeezed ourselves into the crowd headed into the bazaar's front entrance.

Inside were galleries of stalls extended into a blur but we could not stop—people in constant motion pushed from all sides. I tried to stand still and get my bearings but it felt like I was being battered by waves. Tolkuchka lived up to its name as the crowd carried Eileen and me along. My particular spot in the mob must have been the focal point of the "Push Market." So it was for the 14th Century Muslim adventure traveler Ibn Battuta who entered a Turkmen bazaar for the first time and found he could not move in any direction because of the press of people. The locals called it "al-Shawr." Only with "great exertions" did he manage to extract himself.

The fists of an old, short, squat woman in traditional dress and a colored headscarf were shoved into my back for a good twenty yards. She barreled through the crowd with the tenacity of an NFL fullback. The mob spat me out at the margins of the bazaar where I was confronted with a pile of freshly-made branch brooms. Moments later, Eileen, Enrique, and Helen emerged.

"We've found the food court," Enrique said, gesturing at the nearby stalls where women cooked *plov* in giant woks or fried mystery sausages in oil, and men braised *shashliek* (shish-kebab), all of it steaming in the sun. The *shashliek* cooked at the end of long, narrow troughs with hot coals of scrub wood fueling the heat from the opposite end. The dishes were heavy with meat. Wafting scents of grease were mouth-watering.

"Do you want to see some carpets?" Enrique said, reading my mind.

I caught sight of a five-foot stack of carpets to my left and Enrique led us back into the crowd toward the carpets. Successive curtains of pomegranate, crimson, scarlet, and burgundy carpets were displayed over low-slung iron bars buried into the ground, like industrial strength clotheslines. The hanging carpets showed off the vendor's wares while providing a wall of wool that divided the stalls. Vendors folded and stacked the remainder of their inventory into piles. For the eye it was an obstacle course of the red spectrum. A hundred rolls of the best color film could not have captured the richness and subtle variance of red tribal rugs, brown camel bags, yards of rough blue silk, and piles of yellow wool yarn.

We moved down the row, trying not to show too much interest, while at the same time allowing our eyes to adjust. My first response to the carpets, and their medallion-like designs was that it seemed like looking at paintings of modern art—I did not understand them but I knew what I liked. There is an intangible in art that inspires people to rapture. Paint added to canvas in a certain way transforms the two simple materials into something priceless. Wool died and knotted together undergoes a similar transformation. The carpets were works of art with a practical use. The repeating designs had a hypnotic affect. I could feel an irrational urge to posses them, much like what bibliomaniacs must feel for books. Carpet enthusiasts have a name for people with an urge to collect Turkmen carpets: "Turkmaniacs."

Almost all vendors were women, helped by teenage sons dressed western-style in nylon warm-up pants and t-shirts. Gold teeth were common. Originally, gold was used out of dental necessity because of the practice of holding a cube of sugar under the top lip while drinking tea, but it had become fashionable to have all or at least two gold front teeth.

There were a few enticements of "Hey, meester," with a gesture to a carpet by a teenaged son.

Eileen was offered a "war-rug" made in Afghanistan in the 1980's and 1990's to honor the Mujahideen fighters in the war against the Soviets. She knelt down to run her hand across the pile depicting armored personnel carriers, helicopters, rocket-propelled grenades and two large AK-47 assault rifles. While Eileen politely passed on the offer, the carpet reminded me that Taliban-controlled Afghanistan was only 250 miles down the road and shared a 750-mile border with Turkmenistan. The Taliban were recognized by only a handful of countries—one of them Turkmenistan.

At the end of textile row were the hat sellers. Men with their hats arrayed on wire stakes pressed into the ground took a more aggressive approach than the women. One eager young man in his late teens nearly had a wild looking wool *tilpek* hat pressed onto my head before I could find the chance to waive him off. The *tilpeks* looked like a giant shock of gravity-defying dreadlocks. Budget models were wild and unkempt as if they've come right off a scalped sheep. Some smelled of urine. The more expensive *tilpeks* were washed, groomed and shaped with the same care as if they were about to be entered into the Westminster Kennel Club's category for standard poodles. Other hat vendors sold the more traditional-looking Russian *schapkas* made of mink or other furry, non-woolly creatures. No matter what the weather, no matter how hot, older men in the countryside wore either *tilpeks* or *schapkas*.

Turkmenistan was a nation of hats. Headgear served as national or tribal markers. Even the President recognized this. During a televised speech to his cabinet, he instructed all government officials to wear the *takhya*, a close fitting skullcap embroidered with bright interlocking designs. He proclaimed it the national Turkmen headgear. "Let us wear it during festivals and on days of mourning, and at work too. It cannot be bettered," Niyazov said. Whenever I watched Turkmen TV, I saw officials wearing it.

My baseball hat easily marked me as an American. The Turkmen must think of them as part of the American's national headdress. Wearing the baseball hat made me feel the same as if I had worn a red beanie with a propeller and a sandwich board announcing, "I AM AN AMERICAN." I could have explained that the symbols represented different tribes like the Red Sox or the Yankees.

A local hat was *de rigueur* if you wanted to go native. Which type depended on which type of native you wanted to be—Turkmen or ethnic Russian. I saw the flip-side of that behavior in young Turkmen men who wore baseball caps so they could appear American. We could trade identities by trading headgear.

I decided this was the time to buy. Approaching the most wrinkled old man with a white flowing beard and a *tilpek,* I inspected his array of hats with the help of his teenage business associate. The teenager held one of the rarer white *tilpeks* above my head. He placed it on me as if he had just performed a coronation, and held a small shard of mirror up to my face. Even if I felt I looked ridiculous, among Turkmen men it was the norm. Pictures of the fierce tribal khans of the Merv Oasis taken during from the Russian conquest of 1880's showed that *tilpeks* used to be much larger, like a medium-sized beach ball. If nothing else, they increased a Turkmen's profile and may have had added an element of intimidation when confronting potential adversaries.

The teenager quoted an asking price of 200,000 Manat ($10). Bargaining was expected. With facial expressions and a shaking of the head, I tried to feign surprise at the price. Language may have been a barrier but no vendor let that interfere with commerce. The young man instantly produced a small Chinese-made pocket calculator, punched up his price and handed it to me. Numbers were a universal language. After several passes of the calculator making offers and counteroffers, I agreed to 100,000 Manat. All sales in the Bazaar were cash—no credit cards, no checks, just cash. I handed the boy my bills of Manat and he clasped my hand with it, expressing a phrase so quickly that my infantile understanding of Russian did not grasp it. I thought for a second that he was rejecting my offer. He was instead pronouncing a Turkmen blessing on the sale.

Confused but relieved, I tried to make known that I wanted my picture taken with the old man. He became agitated and backed away when I displayed my camera. Had I violated some local custom? Was there some superstitious Turkmen phobia about cameras stealing souls? Enrique later explained to me that the ancient *tilpek* wearers had come to resent having their pictures taken, perhaps feeling the same indignity of a cigar store Indian.

With the transaction at an end, I carried the *tilpek* away in a plastic shopping bag. I lacked the confidence to wear it out of the bazaar. This was a cold weather hat, I rationalized, not meant to be worn under the August sun.

Near the hat sellers, a vendor decided he could interest me in a full-length, yellow leather tribal coat lined and trimmed with karakul, the prized wool of infant sheep still *in utero*. It looked like something that ought to be worn by a shaman. I smiled politely and waved him away.

Pushed again by the crowd, I glimpsed stalls selling fruit, vegetables, fabric, children's or women's clothing, men's shoes, and cauldron-sized aluminum pots. I backtracked through the textiles, looking for Eileen. She was looking at small, conical baby's hats displayed by two women. Each had its own colorful design of rings and interlocking web of geometric patterns. Like snowflakes, no two looked alike. In the 1880's, the English adventurer Henry Landsdell tried to buy a baby's cap but the parents refused saying the child would be ill without it. I showed Eileen my prize hat and we decided that was enough bargaining for the day.

As Enrique and Helen drove us back to the compound, I felt we had stepped outside the artificial Ashgabat. The bazaar had shown me scenes of an authentic Turkmenistan. Shopping in the capital carried little of the colorful barter and truck of Tolkuchka. Where Tolkuchka offered airborne camels, the State-sanctioned bazaars were sterile and limited.

That evening, I overheard Eileen on the phone in her weekly call to her parents.

"I forgot to bring a sun hat for Charlotte and myself," she said.

"You don't have hats!" replied her mother in a heightened state of concern.

My father-in-law, who was on the extension, joined in, "What's the matter, don't they have hats in that country?

If only they knew.

Three weeks later we received a package from Eileen's mother containing six hats for Charlotte and four for Eileen and myself, including a floppy fluorescent pink one and two modified French Foreign Legion-style.

* * *

Tolkuchka was the unvarnished exception to our first days in Ashgabat. The wide boulevards and white marble government buildings we passed daily were kept meticulously swept. President Niyazov was creating a showplace for the outside world. Tolkuchka was everything Ashgabat was not.

Amidst the state-controlled stores and centrally planned economy, Tolkuchka was the Hong Kong of Turkmenistan, where vendors entered into freewheeling bargaining with all comers. Why the Government allowed the bazaar to exist when it suffocated every other small business with state controls and corruption was a mystery. Turkmenistan was the most Soviet authoritarian of the former Soviet Republics. *The Economist* magazine had even dubbed it the worst place to live because of its repressive economic and civil liberties.

The commerce of the bazaar was older than the modern state, and the government knew not to interfere. Once, during cotton harvesting season in the northern city of Dashoguz, the government tried to close the local bazaar and force all the vendors out into the fields to pick cotton. A riot led by the women vendors caused damage to police vehicles and government buildings. The next day, the government reopened the bazaar.

When I told some of my urban Turkmen friends about my fascination with Tolkuchka, they could not understand. Most did not like shopping there and considered it too dirty and chaotic. They preferred the more modern Turkish owned store that recently opened.

"You have such nice modern shopping in America. Why would you want to go to a place like Tolkuchka?" they would say in disbelief.

"Some Americans get tired of the same old malls, where there's nothing unusual," I tried to explain.

By contrast, we had shopped in Ashgabat's more centrally located, state-regulated bazaars. A grocery shop, the most mundane of tasks, might become an opportunity for adventure, taking on the air of a scavenger hunt, but it had none of the excitement of Tolkuchka. One store had long-life milk; another had bread and mops. The combinations were ever changing and unpredictable. If you found something you like—you bought lots of it. This encouraged an obsession to hoard.

The "Mir" or "World" market was one of the Soviet-planned, central bazaars, built as a hard concrete slab floor the size of a football field and sheltered by a high, corrugated metal roof. Underneath was a series of gritty stalls that housed vendors selling fruit and vegetables. Women in long gowns and colorful headscarves managed most of the stands. There was also a meat section where a young man in a bloody butcher's apron tried to entice me with a smile and a wave of his meat axe into buying a skinned sheep carcass. Careful not to offend, I smiled and moved briskly onto the next stall.

"They have bananas!" exclaimed our seasoned American sponsors on our first trip to the Mir. Without a regular supply, I followed our mentor's advice and bought an entire bunch. A woman in a yellow headscarf with a front row of gold teeth sold them to me for 84,000 Manat (about $11 at the official, $4 on the black-market rate).

Piled at the back of the Mir were pyramids of dusty yellow melons the size and shape of footballs. The women vendors wrapped themselves in scarves like pirates and sat on the ground under umbrellas, watching over their piles of melons. Melons could be bought for less than fifty cents each. Melons were grown here since before the time of Alexander the Great. I bought two and carried one under each arm. They were the tastiest, most flavorful melons I had ever eaten. Six hundred and fifty years earlier, the world traveler and geographer, Ibn Battuta, gave the most glowing account possible to the Turkmen melons reporting that they "have no equal in any country of the world, East or West."

Around the corner, a man in the hot sun was selling giant fish from the trunk of his car—no container, no ice—just fish in a trunk. They looked like sturgeon. He must have driven all the way from the shores of the Caspian Sea— about an eight-hour drive. The smell was incredible. Again, I smiled and hurried away.

The scene at the Mir was a middle ground between Tolkuchka and the modern Turkish-owned supermarket, the only one of its kind in the entire country. It was a modern recent addition to Ashgabat, and for the few who could afford its prices, the store provided Turkish imports of food and clothes. The size of the store gave the illusion of variety. Inside, whole aisle sections were stocked with a single item such as cottonseed oil or kilo bags of sugar. Here we shopped for laundry detergent. The leading brand was an Iranian product called, "Barf." We decided to go with a competitor, "Bingo." We also found Kellogg's Rice Krispees with the "Snap" character on the box exhorting something in a cartoon balloon written in Arabic. Eileen, a student of Arabic, assured me Snap was not exclaiming "Death to America!"

Literally at the end of town, set on a rocky plain, was the wholesale market, also known to the locals as the "drinks market." I thought of it as the Turkmen equivalent of a Price Club in a maze of rusting 20-foot sea-land containers. Shrink-wrapped pallets of *Coca-Cola* and Russian beer and vodka were offered for sale in bulk. Things I might have easily turned my nose up at weeks ago became highly prized. Turkish canned goods or Iranian salt were top quality. If it was wine, Moldavian Cabernet was considered the standard. Bulgarian was even better. I bought a bottle of "Mike Tyson Vodka"—it showed his picture on the front flanked by American flags. The vodka was distilled by an unidentified manufacturer but the label described it as a "drink of equality and elegance."

By day's end, we could easily spend 1 million Manat ($200 official rate, $50 unofficial) for our family's weekly grocery needs. Since bill denominations ranged from 50 to 10,000 Manat, I felt like a bagman for the Mafia carrying around shopping bags full of bills.

* * *

Tolkuchka became a regular destination. Even when I knew I would not buy anything, I went for the spectacle. I would find any excuse to go and even volunteered to take others. It was an ideal perch for people-watching. Over time I began to see patterns in the behavior of the vendors and myself.

Like early European merchants must have felt when they walked into a strange bazaar, I saw things that I did not know existed and then decided I needed them. After my first few visits, I took an interest in yurt bands, one-foot by fifty-foot wool bands that wound around the outside of the round tents of Turkmen nomads (yurts or gars) to strengthen them against the desert winds. It was an elaborate latticework of compact, hand-knotted wool pile. Henry Landsdell, the 19th Century English adventurer, had admired their elaborate designs after having seen one cut up into pieces and used as chair backs in the home of the Russian Governor General. Landsdell bargained with poor results, paying dearly for a soiled, second-hand specimen.

The first yurt bands I saw were coiled in the corner of a stall where a woman and her children were selling traditional Turkmen silk dresses and *suzanis*, colorful embroidered cloths more closely identified with the Uzbeks. No effort was made to display them. I smiled at the woman with locks of gray hair falling out of her headscarf and gestured to the spool of textile. She looked confused but put her hand on the yurt band with an expression that said, "You mean this old thing?" I nodded and she unfurled the band in a lackluster fashion.

As soon as I showed an interest, yurt bands came out of all corners of the bazaar and were unrolled at my feet and thrust into my hands with their purveyors quoting lower prices. Arguments broke out among the interlopers apparently trying to decide who had interfered with the other's business. The original vendor became angered at the interlopers, exchanging Turkmen words in a tone that said, "I saw him first, take a hike."

As a foreigner I was expected to be naïve and rich. I drew a crowd of lurkers and other interested shoppers. If I decided to bargain the lurkers would run off to their vendor and report on whatever I was bargaining for. This was the immediacy of the marketplace at work and better than any online auction—I had instant, tangible results. I could also sense a more ominous undercurrent—that some lurkers might be working for the Government reporting on the activities of foreigners.

Among the lurkers, I noticed a small, mouse-like woman standing at my elbow. With her hair up in a traditional Turkmen way, covered by a canary-yellow floral scarf, she was no taller than my chest. She could hear my disastrous attempts to communicate in Russian.

"It would be my pleasure to assist you," she said in a soft voice with a slight British accent. Her diminutive size and childlike appearance were disarming. She introduced herself as Shemshat, a kindergarten teacher of English who comes to the bazaar, she said, to look for foreigners so she could practice her conversational English. Would I mind if she followed me around?

"No, I'd welcome it," I said, relieved to have the skills of an interpreter at my side. She kept a calm demeanor as she helped me close a deal on the yurt band. She must be wondering, "What was this crazy American doing buying yurt bands? Does he have his own yurt in the United States?"

We looked at more hats. I measured my bargaining skills against *tilpek* hats. I bought six from the same old man, getting a better price per hat each time. I grew cocky thinking that by the time I left Turkmenistan, that maybe he would pay me to take a *tilpek*.

Whatever Shemshat thought, she remained unfazed by the demands of my quirky shopping spree. Her response as I completed each transaction was always the same: "Now what would you like to see?"

With my collection of hats and yurt bands, I said, "I think I'm finished for today." I thanked her and thought about how I would explain the yurt bands to Eileen.

The lurker effect could also backfire. When some lurkers ascertained that I was interested in old things, one vendor, acting on this information, pointed to a carpet I was examining and said that it was maybe 150 or 200 years old. Even to my untrained eye, I guessed it was closer to 15 or 20 years old. When I went to look for cooking pots for a friend, a large woman, flashing a gold smile, assured me through pantomime that one of her pots was buried in the ground for a long time before she unearthed it.

* * *

Carpets were at the heart of the Turkmen people and, not surprisingly, at the heart of Tolkuchka. Textiles were what Marco Polo most remembered about his journey through the region. "Look at a man's carpets and you look at a man's soul," went a Turkmen saying. The national window on the soul was Ashgabat's National Carpet Museum that housed a priceless collection of antique tribal carpets and textiles. Some weeks after our first Tolkuchka visit, Eileen, Charlotte and I visited the museum, where we each had to exchange our shoes for a one-size-(does not)-fit-all set of fuzzy house slippers. My heels awkwardly hung out the back.

While we shuffled along the carpeted floors in our fuzzy house slippers, I tried to absorb the intricacies of the many carpet styles and techniques. The exhibit halls were as lifeless as a mausoleum except for the two dozing women at the front door who had sold us our chits. Charlotte was more interested in her new slippers than in any of the centuries-old textiles. The centerpiece of the museum was the world's largest handmade carpet, measuring 32 x 60 feet, hanging in a special multi-story room. In keeping with the Soviet fascination for all things gigantic, the carpet was woven in just seven months in 1941 and intended to be a decorative backdrop for Moscow's Bolshoi Theater. It was returned when it proved to be too heavy for the theater's supports. When the Soviets collectivized carpet weaving, they turned a practical Turkmen handicraft into an industry. The mobile nomadic looms of the steppe had been replaced by horizontal looms of iron pipe organized in carpet "factories." Rugs that had been woven for reasons of necessity, in tribal patterns passed down from mother to daughter, were discarded and replaced by rugs based on political designs like the face of Lenin.

With the Turkmen weaver's reputation for the most densely knotted wool carpets in the world, I estimated that the hanging behemoth weighed well over several tons. Steel cables suspended the giant carpet. If the supports gave way, the weight of the falling carpet could easily be enough to at least smother my entire family, if not crush us to death.

* * *

After the demise of the Soviets, Tolkuchka carpet sellers had sold political designs only as novelties and instead reverted to selling traditional tribal patterns with an overlay of capitalism. Competition and intrigue among the carpet sellers was fierce. Unflattering rumors were started by one seller about a competitor. If one seller would see me looking at another's carpets, she would whisper things like, "she overcharges" or "she washes her carpets to make them look old."

The carpet sellers did not miss an opportunity to make a sale even during a rare snowstorm. Rather than spread their carpets on the ground to be covered by the falling snow, several boys wore carpets on their backs like heavy cloaks and paraded up and down the stalls hoping to lure customers.

One carpet seller named Guljahan was introduced to me by an Embassy colleague who had been in the country for two years. She held one of the more prominent stalls on textile row. In her early forties, already a grandmother several times over, Guljahan first started coming to Tolkuchka about twenty years ago when she was making and selling hand-knotted carpets to help support her family. Her manner was not aggressive; rather, she approached customers with an almost shy smile and pleasant demeanor. Behind this initial impression of modesty was a quiet confidence. Guljahan knew the quality of her carpets would bring customers back. Unlike many of her competitors, she recognized the importance of building a good reputation. Guljahan's low-pressure sales technique worked to bring me back to her stall more than any other of the carpet sellers.

We visited her stall on a brilliant October morning, as beautiful as any fall weather I could remember growing up in the Midwest—60's, sunshine, and a small flotilla of white fluffy clouds pushed by a slight breeze along a sparkling blue sky. It would have been perfect football weather had we been at a Big Ten stadium on a Saturday afternoon.

Guljahan's brothers and sons "threw" carpets for us to look at. Successions of designs were unfurled at my feet as her daughter served us weak green tea. The young men unfurled the stacks of red wool in a fluid motion that ended with an audible snap, like a flag in a stiff breeze. It was the carpet's own sound, as if announcing itself. Guljahan's sons would gently turn the carpet at different angles to show off the different hues of red under the Turkmen sun.

Guljahan spoke Russian but preferred Turkmen. Through Eileen's rough translation we learned how she started her business.

"I was a young woman, just married, when I sold my first carpet to a vendor," she began. "It was one that took me months to make. I saw it the next day in the bazaar and how much he marked it up. I decided I should start selling the carpets myself and then organized other women in my village to make carpets."

Guljahan would set out the night before from her village some 65 miles away and arrive at the gates of Tolkuchka in the black, pre-dawn hours to be among the first to set up a stall. Prime location, no different than the need to have a prime location at the local shopping mall, was important to sales. Her determination and persistence worked over time to earn her one of the best locations among the carpet sellers.

Guljahan now regularly made trips to her home village to supervise the work of the women she employed to weave carpets. A couple of times, I was lucky enough to be invited on her quality control trips to her carpet factories. The villages were in remote areas with the shadow of the Kopet Dag on one side and the vast horizon of the Kara Kum Desert on the other. The settlements were little more than a collection of sandstone or mud wall houses where we were greeted by small flocks of Alabai puppies. The factories turned out to be a room of a house. I entered to see three traditionally dressed women leaning intently over fine strands of wool stretched on a horizontal loom made of steel pipe. A bare bulb dangled from the ceiling lit the room.

The women plucked the wool warps with amazing speed and dexterity, as if they were playing a giant harp in unison. They applied colored thread to the skeleton of the warp to leave behind a compact pile of brilliant colors. Red represented blood, which stood for life. White stood for moonlight.

For Guljahan and other women in her village, carpet making was second nature (in Turkmen society men did not make carpets). They never stopped to consult a pattern of the intricate design that was forming. The pattern of their tribe had been imprinted in their memory early in life. They knew by rote how many knots of each color to use and its placement in the pattern. All the while, the women casually exchanged village gossip and jokes. After a certain number of knots, the women used metal comb-like tools with long tines to tighten the knots into place. The motion was both graceful and forceful with the energy of a hammer blow.

The hammering made a rhythmic sound like drums warming up for a tribal dance.

I watched Guljahan inspect a carpet using a tape measure to check the width at different sections. Her demeanor turned to one of a strict school marm as she gave instructions to the women in a no-nonsense tone of voice. Guljahan was known for the quality of her carpets and clearly she wanted to keep standards up. As insurance, black-and-white strands of wool that looked like small snakes were placed on the skeleton of the carpet to ward off the evil eye. The finished carpet would often have a small strand of black-and-white that would continue to protect the carpet.

Watching the women work, I asked one of them to slow down so that I could see exactly how she was tying the knots with their fingers. I had to ask the young woman several times to slow her movements enough until I could actually see the knot she was tying. The labor involved was no less than incredible. At a rate of 10,000 knots per day, two experienced women working ten hours a day, every day, took about four months to complete a four-foot by six-foot carpet. The money the women made was often the only steady income for the village.

"It is easier to dig a hole in the sand with the point of a needle than it is to weave a carpet," Guljahan said, quoting another Turkmen saying.

Despite the fact the carpets were no longer woven by nomadic tribes out of necessity, a woman's ability to weave still had a central place in their life. In the typical Turkmen home, the entire floor was covered with carpets and very little furniture, maybe a wooden chest for storing clothes. The carpets were still woven for personal use, as wedding dowries, as gifts for special visitors, and of course to sell at Tolkuchka.

The rugs, pronounced national treasures by the Government, provided a window into Turkmen life. Each rug carried its own tribal symbol or *gul* (Persian for flower). The five tribes still represented include: Tekkes, the Yomuts, Salor, the Ersari, and the Chodor. The tribes had warred and united with each other over centuries. Some, like the aristocratic but extinct Salor, were defeated over a century ago but their designs were adopted by surviving tribes. The *kejebbeb* designs looked as if they were jewels strung in a line and were specially woven for weddings. Even after seventy years of Soviet rule, tribal identities were deeply ingrained.

Learning the tribal designs was the analytical side of understanding an art form. On the other side was their intangible quality. Individual carpets took on a personality. Depending on the light and at which end they were viewed, the carpets might shift between brownish and salmon. Their character could change. They affected me like people and my interest could be fickle. Carpets I was first attracted to, I lost interest in when I met other carpets.

How was it that objects of intricate design and expressive color were created in surroundings of utter bleakness? Guljahan's small village was on the edge of thousands of square miles of the barren Kara Kum Desert. It was as if the rich hues of the carpets were created to compensate for the lack of color in the landscape. The rugs were not representational but geometric designs floating in fields of red, framed like paintings inside multiple borders.

The carpets from this remote village found their way to Tolkuchka and even to other Central Asian countries as well as Istanbul and Europe. Carpets carried with them an entire world. Even in America where we expect to pay what the price tag says, carpets were bought through the centuries old tradition of bargaining. It is the commercial world of the carpet that controls the price. Despite the fact that exporting carpets out of Turkmenistan was extremely difficult, this was the modern Silk Road still at work.

As we got to know Guljahan and her family, we felt more comfortable with bargaining. There seemed to be two classes of customers at Tolkuchka: locals and the rare foreigner. Because Guljahan knew I lived in Turkmenistan for nearly two years and started to refer others to her, my status fell somewhere in between.

Eileen and I were honored one night when Guljahan invited us to her apartment to be served a Turkmen dinner of *shashliek* and *plov* (rice mixed with fat and vegetables). After dinner, Guljahan served weak green tea while Eileen and I watched a ritual similar to the one in Tolkuchka—her sons threw carpets in her living room for our inspection. Owing to Turkmen superstition, it was the least favorable time to make a sale. Any money that changed hands would have to be done on the floor. To hold the money up in plain sight invited the specter of the evil eye, which could result in the loss of the money.

* * *

I once had a college professor who said that if you could only give one book to space aliens to understand American culture, it should be a *Sears, Roebuck and Co.* catalog. In the same way, Tolkuchka could explain Turkmen culture. This was where Turkmen revealed their true nature—a tribal character unchanged for millennia.

JOURNEY 4

Ancient Merv: The Heart of the Silk Road

We came in view of an immense wilderness of ruined buildings,
forming a semicircle in front of us to the north and south.
--Edmund O'Donovan, The Merv Oasis, 1882

To know the heart of Turkmenistan, you have to know the ancient city of Merv. Once heralded as "Queen of the Ancient World," it rivaled Baghdad as a center of Islamic art, culture, and learning. Merv's position between the great civilizations of East and West fixed it squarely in the path of the West's greatest empire builder, Alexander the Great, and the East's greatest empire destroyer, Genghis Khan. Alexander and Ghengis Khan were like bookends to Merv's noble history with the trade routes known as the Silk Road. Since the abrupt end of its golden age at the hands of the Mongols in the early 13th Century, nature had buried its acres of desiccated remains under the sands of the Kara Kum Desert, leaving only the nearby Russian-founded city of Mary (pronounced Mer-REE). After our first year in Ashgabat, Eileen and I were fortunate enough to be invited to a rural village outside Mary by a young Turkmen friend, Dovelet. From Dovelet's family home, we hoped to venture out for a look at the ruins of Merv.

* * *

The name Merv is full of myth. It is a primordial pool for religion, a mixing bowl for leaning and commerce, and a strategic point for military strategy. Believed in Hindu and Arab traditions to be the ancient site of paradise, it has also been said to be the place where Scheherezade told the stories of the *Thousand and One Nights*. According to legend, Prince Zoroaster, a native of lands that are now Afghanistan, founded his fire-based religion in the Merv oasis along the banks of the Murgap River.

To the Greeks, Merv was originally known as Margiana—the margin of the known world. In 331 BC, Alexander the Great found Merv's oasis an excellent location to garrison his troops following their victory over King Darius of Persia. From Merv, Alexander's army launched the farthest-reaching of his campaigns against the Bactrian Kingdom into what is modern-day Afghanistan. Alexander's General Selucus, better known as the founder of the Selucid dynasty, understood its position as a crossroads linking China and India with the Mediterranean and the western world. Selucus developed Merv as a center for commerce. Trade along the routes of the Silk Road began to flourish.

In the early centuries after Christ, the Silk Road brought Buddhists monks and then Christian missionaries to Merv. Merv became the center of learning for the Nestorians, a branch of Christianity that survives today in Jordan and Iraq. The Silk Road continued to bring trade. Merchants traded Ferghana horses or ox-blood colored carpets for silk threads or spices newly arrived from the east. Caravans traveling east from Merv could journey along a northern route to Tajikistan, through the Pamirs, to Western China, Kashgar, and on to Peking, where they traded large-bulb onions and iron tools for lacquer and jade ornaments. Caravans moving south through Afghanistan could trade for the riches of India. In the 8th Century, Merv was made the Capital of Khorasan (a kingdom covering northern and eastern Iran up to the Amudarya River).

The Seljuk Turks, who ruled the city in the 11th Century, recognized that water was the key to the city's prosperity, and built a dam and an elaborate system of canals on the Murgap River. So long as there was water, Merv would thrive. Merv again became a center for religious learning—this time Islam. Dozens of mosques and madrasses filled the city. Sultan Sanjar, a Seljik Emperor, sponsored a 150,000-volume library.

In 1221, however, Merv's vibrant life was extinguished by the full destructive power of Ghengis Khan. The Mongol conqueror dispatched the most brutal of his generals, his youngest son Toloui, to conquer Merv. Toloui's army razed the city and its ornate palaces and burned its great libraries. The Arab geographer, Yakut, one of the few residents of Merv to flee before the Horde, wrote that Merv's grand buildings "were effaced from the earth as lines of writing are effaced from paper." Men, women, and children were separated and distributed in herds to the battalions, and systematically beheaded. Toloui's own estimate put the entire number killed at a conservative 500,000. Islamic historians put the number at 700,000—a bloody massacre even by Ghengis Khan's standards.

Following the Mongols, Merv fell into obscurity. The Turkmen themselves have no written history of their own for this time but legend tells the tale of the surviving Turkmen; scattered into the wastes of the Kara Kum Desert. Some migrated to the Anatolian Peninsula where the Seljuks (descendants themselves of the earliest Turkmen from the central Asian steppe) gave them land, and they laid the foundations to the Ottoman Empire that emerged two centuries

later. The Mongols and other groups tried to govern the remaining Turkmen tribes but found them unbowed. In the
centuries that followed the destruction of Merv, the Turkmen branched out into twenty-three major tribes.

By 1870, the most dominant of the tribes was the Tekke.
They took possession of the Ahal region in south-central
Turkmenistan and the Merv Oasis then branched into two
sub-tribes, known by their geographic location: the Ahal
Tekke and the Merv Tekke.

In 1884, proud and independent to the end, the Merv
Tekkes were the last group to submit to Russia's conquest
of Central Asia. Their cousins, the Ahal Tekkes, had just
suffered a terrible military defeat including the massacre of
thousands of women and children at Geok Tepe. When the
Merv Tekkes finally surrendered the Merv Oasis, the Russians founded nearby Mary and built a train station for their
Trans-Caspian Railroad. Even now, in post-Soviet Turkmenistan, the Merv Tekke's independent streak makes them sus-
pect in the eyes of President Niyazov.

* * *

After a year of a friendship with Dovelet, he invited us to
visit his village outside the provincial city of Mary. Turkmen
are very private, clannish, and wary of outsiders, so when
Dovelet extended the invitation, we felt we had crossed an
important threshold of trust. Unlike the more gregarious
Arab world, an invitation to eat with a Turkmen in the family
home was not made lightly. Dovelet also had to be cautious
because the Government would take particular interest in
anyone who visited with foreigners, particularly those associated with the American Embassy. The family was the most
valued part of Turkmen life.

Dovelet was unusual for a Turkmen. He lived and worked
in the capitol city of Ashgabat but came from a small agricultural village. He was proud of his tribal heritage as a

member of the Merv branch of the Tekke tribe. At the same time, he had worldly interests; showed talent for painting and music; and spoke Arabic, English, German, and French. Dovelet aspired to study in the United States and to work for the United Nations. He and his two younger brothers were raised by a single mother who had been a schoolteacher and had divorced her husband, something almost unheard of in Turkmen society. Usually it was the husband who divorced his wife. She was also one of the first women in Mary to drive her own car.

* * *

On a May morning, Eileen and I set out from Ashgabat to follow the eastward route of the Silk Road to Merv. Charlotte remained in Elena's care. Instead of breaking down our yurts and loading our camels, we pulled the Jeep into the back alley of Dovelet's Soviet block apartment building. Dovelet and his wife, Jennet, their six-year-old daughter, Sanja, and their three-year-old son, Yousef, squeezed into the back seat. Jennet, dressed in a traditional long Turkmen dress and a headscarf, kept a serene smile on her face, and I judged how our day was going by whether her smile was still there. Sanja was shy with fair skin and a thick head of chestnut hair. Yousef held a gleam of mischief in his eye and climbed all over the inside of the Jeep, chattering away in Turkmen and repeating the only English he seemed to know, "Jeep John, Jeep John." He wanted to climb onto my lap and look out the front window as I drove.

"How did you two meet?" Eileen asked Dovelet while trying to include Jennet into the conversation.

"Jennet was from the next village," Dovelet said. "Her tribe was different, so her parents would not accept me."

He said that the custom was for the suitor's family to visit the woman's family and wait as the man presented them with a plate of cookies and biscuits. If the platter was returned with the cookies rearranged, the family accepted the man. If the cookies were untouched, the man was rejected.

"The first two times, her parents would not touch the platter," Dovelet said looking coyly at Jennet. "On the third time, her parents rearranged the cookies."

Dovelet had been refused because his future wife's family belonged to a distinct sub-tribe of the Tekke called the "Bokaz." The father-in-law had wanted his daughter to take a husband from within their tribe even though it had a lower status than Dovelet's. According to Tekke folklore, the ancestor of the Bokaz was an abandoned child whom the Tekke adopted into their tribe generations ago, but whose descendants still maintained a separate identity from that of the main Tekke tribe.

As we drove out of the eastern edge of Ashgabat, Dovelet advised that we should fill up with gas before leaving the city limits. Mary, Dovelet explained, was the President's least favorite of the five *velyats* or provincial districts. At the same time Sanja began to cry, saying she had a stomach ache.

"Our people are the most independent," Dovelet said. "This is considered a threat to the President's authority. We have a reputation for being successful entrepreneurs. We make a lot of consumer trade with our Iranian neighbors. As punishment, it was rumored that the President often shorted Mary on gas and other rations."

We met the first checkpoint about fifty miles outside of Ashgabat. Travel in and out of the capital zone was strictly controlled by permit. With the Jeep's blue diplomatic license plates, the border guards eyed us warily and then waved us around the checkpoint barriers.

Sanja's crying continued, and she seemed so miserable that I offered to turn around and make the four-hour drive another day. Dovelet said that this was her usual response to riding in a car for any length of time. We pulled over to let her be sick. She eventually fell asleep with her head cradled in Dovelet's lap.

As we drove past cotton fields with their unlined irrigation ditches, Dovelet said, "You know I'm a country boy," and then laughed at himself. With the transition in landscape, Dovelet's demeanor relaxed.

We passed through the town of Tedjen, the halfway point to Mary. At both towns' gas stations, lines of cars waited to fill their tanks.

On the far side of Tedjen, a man sat in a broken, backless chair at a makeshift roadside stand. He seemed to be offering for sale a half-filled bottle of brown liquid. The bottle sat in the sun on a teetering stool. It was either an example of the most pathetic or the most entrepreneurial person we had seen in Turkmenistan—I couldn't tell which. Out of pure curiosity, I was half-tempted to stop and ask him what he was selling. My romance of the Silk Road was dying hard.

* * *

By early afternoon, we had crossed the nearly dry Murgap River south of Mary, and turned off the paved road onto a dirt road that leads to Dovelet's village. We had covered in four hours what might have taken a camel caravan four days in the 19th Century.

"This is where I feel strongest," Dovelet said. "I want to move back here one day."

Dovelet's passion for his tribal village disproved the theory of "Soviet Man"—a mythical citizen devoid of all cultural ties, whose only loyalty was to the State, an idea propagated by the Soviet Union. Turkmen love their country—from the determined Christians who chose to remain in Turkmenistan and practice their religion; to the exchange student who returned after a year in the U.S.; to the cultured, western-oriented intellectual struggling to make a decent life for his family.

The village was a series of one-story, dust-yellow brick houses. There were no street signs or traffic lights or pictures of the President. House fronts were lined in the traditional way with high walls facing the street. Backyards were filled with gardens, fruit trees, sheep, and usually a lone camel.

Dovelet directed us to the side courtyard of what had been his mother's house. By tradition, it now belonged to Dovelet's youngest brother. The youngest offspring inherit the parents' property, a tradition shared or borrowed from the Mongols. Dovelet's mother had died of hepatitis only a few years before at the age of forty-five. In his late twenties, Dovelet was the oldest of the three boys and, as the senior male in his family, was now viewed as the patriarch. He was relied upon for advice and guidance, particularly to his two younger brothers. The brothers had started a small business importing motor oil from Iran to service the influx of gray-market Japanese cars into Mary.

His two brothers and their families and several of Dovelet's aunts greeted us. Eileen and I removed our shoes and were led inside to a room covered with tribal carpets. We were served a lunch of melons, grapes, *plov*, soup, and compote. Dovelet introduced his brothers, their wives, and their children. Another aunt from next door joined the group with her children.

The women of the household observed the Turkmen custom of *yashmak*, which proscribes that women cover their mouths with their headscarves when senior relations are present out of respect and modesty. This could be in the presence of female or male relations. The wives of Dovelet's younger brothers had to cover their mouths in the presence of Dovelet. This was not based on Islam, but was part of an elaborate system of Turkmen cultural rules that governed family relationships. The young daughters-in-law did not address the older males or females in the household directly. If one of the women wanted to say something to her in-laws, she had to convey it through a child in the house who would tell the in-law adult. There was a hierarchy to this. Dovelet's wife did not have to cover her mouth because Dovelet was the senior man in the household. The young wives did not try to communicate directly to either Eileen or myself, but instead tried to make themselves as scarce as possible. Even during meals, they made a point of holding their scarves up around their faces—eating behind them.

A television in the corner tuned to the official government television station showed the President walking down a red carpet sprinkled with rose petals, welcoming foreign dignitaries. They were met by a troupe of teenage girls who presented loaves of bread and performed a brief dance routine.

"It has never been the custom for Turkmen women to dance in front of strange men like that," Dovelet said.

Eileen and I saw female folk dancing troupes on the two government-run channels whenever the President received officials at the airport or during official celebrations.

"To a traditional Turkmen father it would be shameful to send a daughter to greet an unknown man."

Even the few billboards in Ashgabat seemed to profane Turkmen traditions. The large silver headdresses seen on Turkmen women in advertisements for detergent or baby food, apparently portraying the average Turkmen housewife, made the ads look ridiculous, as the headgear would be worn only by the richest women during a wedding ceremony and certainly not while doing housework. These were examples of how the Soviet Union tried to reform Turkmenistan into a socialist secular society, modifying traditional symbols. In a Russian context this might have made sense. Folk dancing girls offering bread to visitors is a Slavic custom, not a Turkmen one. After Turkmen independence, President Niyazov seemed to have become more Soviet than the Soviets and in the process continued to turn Turkmen traditions into state-manipulated stereotypes.

Traditional family ties were much more pronounced in Mary. Dovelet made so many introductions to aunts, uncles, and cousins that I felt we were part of a bad play. Driving the muddy ruts of his village, he could always point out yet another uncle's home. I got the sense that "uncle" may have been an all-purpose word for any extended relation like a second or third cousin.

I finally asked him, "Are you related to the whole village?"

"Yes, I think so," he replied in all earnestness.

* * *

The rest of the day turned into a cavalcade of visits to the homes of relatives. We drove into Mary to call on the senior members of his extended family. There was Murdan, the patriarch and Dovelet's senior uncle. He presented us with an array of Turkmen soups, mutton, *plov*, vegetables, and fruits. Uncle Murdan was a senior level official in the Mary *Hakeem's* office. Dovelet sought his advice and blessings for family and business decisions.

The oldest member of the extended family was his great aunt who, despite her gender, trumped the normally male-dominated family. Even though she was widowed and without children, seemingly a bad position to be in, Dovelet referred to her as "head of the clan," and she clearly commanded the most respect. She sat with her silk Turkmen robes and woolen slippers while younger relatives served us tea, and children played behind her. Her uncut gray hair was worn in a bun. Her face was lined, but she expressed a gentle manner as if she was comfortable with life. As a young woman, she would have held the least authority in the family. Now, she commanded the greatest deference. I wondered if this reverence for the old woman set Turkmen society apart from other Islamic societies such as the Arabs of the Middle East.

We had barely sipped one cup of green tea when Dovelet—intent on having us meet as many relations as possible—announced that we had to leave to meet another relative. This was not the Turkmen way, as visits would traditionally last hours or even days to show guests the appropriate hospitality.

Dovelet led us on to the home of the youngest brother's father-in-law, one of Turkmenistan's most well-known artists. Even though the brother had been married almost a year, by custom, he still could not visit his father-in-law until he had given his father-in-law some large scale present—almost like a reverse dowry. *Kalong* they called it, meaning bride's price. The bride's family demanded a huge sum of money from the groom in return for marriage. We let him out of the car about a block before we came to the house. He would wait while we would visit.

"I had to wait two years before I had saved enough money to buy my in-laws their gift," Dovelet said.

"It seems like a sweet custom," said Eileen. "It allows the parents time to still have their daughter to themselves. Time to get used to letting her go."

The father-in-law artist, Maksat, was a gregarious bear-like man in his fifties. Maksat's house seemed much more like a traditional dwelling of the Middle East. It was more beautiful and soothing than anything we had encountered in the wholesome but hardscrabble countryside so far. Maksat clearly took delight in ushering us into his large walled-in backyard. It was a tamed jungle of some twenty varieties of fruit trees and flowers. His compound held two guesthouses, painted in bright colors with mosque-like designs, and had two domes. We were shown to a long table with benches lined with bowls of fruit, plates of nuts, raisins, and cookies; dishes of *plov*, lamb, and cucumbers. Dinner was served with vodka toasts. Maksat, like many Turkmen, was not a strict Muslim. During the meal, he produced a platinum bowl studded with jewels given to him by Benizer Bhutto, former Prime Minister of Pakistan, as a token of her appreciation for painting her portrait. He decided we should drink vodka out of the bowl. We passed it around, like members of a toastmaster's meeting, with each one of us trying to offer up our best wishes for the moment.

"To our hosts and the health of Benizer Bhutto," I found myself saying as the cup was passed to me for my turn for a toast.

Maksat's daughter arrived to visit her father, the same one who had covered her face at Dovelet's family house. Here, she did not have to observe the *yashmuk* custom and freely moved around her father's house without being subservient.

Maksat offered us a tour of his private gallery chocked full with antique Turkmen crafts, daggers, his favorite paintings, and media clippings of his past success. He picked up a brochure of his own art, scrawled his autograph on it, and handed it to me with the same flourish as if he had been a magnanimous rock star bestowing a gift to a star-struck groupie.

It was approaching ten o'clock and Eileen and I had reached our saturation point for socializing, but Dovelet insisted that we attend another uncle's party—his fiftieth birthday party. I was beginning to feel like an exotic pet Dovelet wanted to show off to his family. We picked up his brother, who had been waiting all this time around the corner, and drove into downtown Mary. Driving through Mary, there were far fewer billboard photos of the President than in Ashgabat.

On the second floor of a Soviet-style concrete building, we were ushered upstairs to a long table overflowing with food that had been sitting for an indeterminate amount of time. We were seated at the men's table for our fourth dinner of the evening.

There was another toast to the birthday uncle, and Eileen and I were informed that we must appear before a crowd of guests on a dance floor and make a toast to the birthday uncle. Dovelet was insistent and to say no would have clearly offended our Turkmen hosts. He firmly guided us to the dance floor, and we were handed microphones. While we looked out onto the crowd, someone turned on a blinding video camera light. Eileen and I took turns stammering something about our best wishes for the uncle with me forgetting the uncle's name.

The next moment, the uncle's daughter requested me to dance. I found this was particularly untraditional as one of the uncle's daughters led me out onto the dance floor. Eileen was left to watch. Still dressed in the same sweaty t-shirt, stained cargo pants, and dirty boots that I had worn since the morning's four-hour drive, I imagined an announcer's voice in my head bellowing to the guests, "Representing the United States, the slovenly guy in sweaty clothes." I staggered around the dance floor, struggling to complete one dance of what seemed like an endless, repetitive, three-note beat. The bass from the speakers vibrated with such force, it should have been able to bore holes through concrete block. Surprisingly, after this group dance, the daughter asked again that I dance. Eileen was not having a brilliant time. In such situations, there was always a concern to be a good sport and not to offend your foreign hosts so I danced, but in the back of my mind I had vague concerns that this meant something irrevocable by Turkmen custom. I imagined the clan's matriarch would appear and announce to the crowd, "The man dances two times with the woman who asks two times—now they are married." How would I explain this to Eileen? "Honey, it's like this...I danced twice and now I'm married. You'll always be number one."

The evening felt as if it had taken on its own out-of-control momentum. Eileen and I decided it was time to leave.

Later, at Dovelet's house, his younger brothers said through Dovelet, without any trace of sarcasm: "Your dancing was beautiful."

This had been our introduction to the modern Tekke tribe. Dovelet promised us tomorrow that we would see ancient Merv.

* * *

The next morning we drove into Mary to visit the Archeological Museum of ancient Merv and hired a guide. A diorama in the Museum showed Merv as a sprawling site. Merv actually contains the remains of five ancient cities. Water had been the key to Merv. It was initially a garden oasis on the banks of the Murgap, but the river kept shifting course. Merv had constantly been rebuilt to follow its path.

Our guide was a young Turkmen, twenty-three years old, who (as soon as he found out we were American), was more interested in talking about his year as a high school exchange student in Oklahoma than ancient Merv.

"I liked Oklahoma," he said. "The people were friendly, and the land reminded me of my home country."

A former student of English at Turkmen State University, he dressed in an American style, complete with a "Hugo Boss" baseball cap. As a guide he earned the equivalent of fifteen dollars a month.

"There are better opportunities in Ashgabat for English speakers," he said. "But I can't apply to the central government to live there until I have spent several years working here in my hometown."

Timur guided our Jeep to an open plain, past heavily irrigated cotton fields, to the base of a man-made hill that overlooked the expanse of ruins.

"This is the heart of Merv," he said, with little ceremony.

Looking at the low, lumpy mounds of dirt and sand, it almost seemed like a poor joke. This was the site where the Queen of the Ancient World had thrived, a city of mythic proportions, but we could have easily driven past without realizing it.

We parked and Timur led us to the top of the hill that had been part of the fortifications of Merv's first city, Erk Kala. It was textured like a petrified dumpling with creases and folds carved into the sides. We parked the Jeep at the base and hiked to the top.

From the top of the hill, Timur explained, "lookouts could be used to watch for dust clouds of approaching caravans or hostile armies."

Through the haze, Timur pointed to Merv's most famous building, the Sultan Sanjar Mausoleum, a mile away. The color of sand, its prominent dome had once been a brilliant azure—supposedly visible to caravans a day's journey away. Its silhouette was all that remained of Merv's skyline. The building jutted from the flat desert horizon, its grand door-way appearing as a small black dot, absorbing all light. A thousand years ago, the Seljik Sultan Sanjar brought Merv to the peak of its golden age. He had the building construct-ed in 1140 as his burial chamber. I tried hard to imagine the vibrant life surrounding it—the mansions, mosques, and Sanjar's grand library. Merv exceeded Damascus in size at the same time Moscow was only a collection of dreary huts. The best architects of the day had designed the mausoleum so well that it was the only building to withstand the full destructive power of the Mongol's war machine, as well as devastating earthquakes and almost nine-hundred scorching summers under the desert sun.

"That's our next stop," said Timur.

We scrambled down the hill and drove dirt roads to the giant mausoleum. Up close, the massive building was haunting, almost menacing, alone on the landscape. A ten-year-old boy charged us 5,000 Manat (between twenty cents and one dollar) to enter. Inside, the domed ceiling rose one hundred feet. The vast space created circulated cool air and a sense of calm, much like the feeling of standing inside the Lincoln memorial. A flock of black birds that had been hiding in the top scattered out of one of the high openings. It was easy to imagine that in ancient times a priest of one of Merv's many religions would have interpreted this as an omen. At the center of the stone floor was an opening in what looked like a well. About twelve feet down was brickwork forming a large rectangle said to be the burial chamber of Sultan Sanjar.

After nine-hundred years, Merv's most visible remnant was a monument to its greatest ruler. Comparing Ashgabat, it was hard not to conclude that the President was trying to emulate the same symbolic immortality. In ten years, President Niyazov had built grand monuments of white marble for the third, fifth, ninth, and tenth anniversaries of Turkmenistan and adorned them with gold statues of himself. He was a man in a hurry to be immortalized every few years. Blue and green domes like that of Sultan Sanjar Mausoleum topped his presidential palace and the Majlis. A thousand years from now, would these imposing structures be all that remained of Ashgabat? Tourists and historians might view it with the same reverence in which we now walked through Sultan Sanjar. The president could link himself to Merv's greatest ruler hoping his name would be remembered as long as Sultan Sanjar's.

We adjusted to the light of the outside, and Timur kept up a steady pace, leading us to the small fortress of Kys Kala and its unusual crenellated mud walls, which were supposedly designed to help deflect missiles from enemy catapults. Kys Kala had been a gift from a Sassanian governor to his daughter, but was later turned into a party palace by Sultan

Sanjar. He hosted lavish parties with female slaves and powerful officials for guests. A large hole in one of its mud walls presented the desert scenery outside as if it was a painting displayed in an oval picture frame.

Timur guided us along to a nearby holy site, the Mosque of Mohammed ibn Said, a Muslim saint from the 12th Century, and an adjacent Madrassa. Ibn Said was the founder of the Shiite Sect of Islam, but this was not his resting place. Like much of the confusing and even conflicting history of Central Asia, this was said to be the actual resting place of a Sunni Imam, Mohammed ibn Hannab. As we approached the Mosque, we overheard whispers out of the darkness of the Madrassa's colonnades. A local Imam was quietly giving instruction to three young men. Independent religious instruction was something unusual to witness in Turkmenistan, as it was under the strict control of the government. Indeed, a month before, the Government had closed down the last remaining Madrassa in Dashaguz, near the border with Uzbekistan.

Behind the Mosque was a holy site lined with low hanging saxaul trees—ubiquitous throughout Turkmenistan—and adorned with ribbons of white cloth. These represented wishes made every year calling upon the holy spirit of the place. The caretakers of the site were a family of at least three generations who made their home in a house carved out of living rock. The youngest member, a three-year-old boy, ran up to us, grinned and unabashedly thrust out his dripping ice cream cone to offer us a taste. Through Dovelet, we introduced ourselves to the boy's proud family and posed for pictures with them. The patriarch of the family directed that I put my arm around the matriarch, a tough weathered woman under five feet in height who was somewhere between sixty and one-hundred. We posed for group photos before going back to Dovelet's village to pack.

* * *

On our drive back to Ashgabat we saw the same man in the same location tending to his half-filled bottle of brown liquid. It was as if he had not moved. I left the dust of Merv without feeling any direct connection between the ancient traders of the Silk Road and the modern tribal Turkmen that lived in nearby Mary. They seemed somewhere in the middle between the golden age of Sultan Sanjar and President Niyazov's highly stylized version of Turkmenistan's announced *Altyn Asyr* or golden age.

The visit to Mary did, however, make the normally omnipresent visage of President Niyazov seem very far away. Niyazov had caricatured the most sensitive aspects of Turkmen culture for his own ends. While he portrayed himself as the leader of all Turkmen and exploited traditions in his attempt to build a national identity, it was obvious to those outside of the capital who practice these traditions that this was not consistant with his own culture.

* * *

Months later, I returned alone to Dovelet's village on a second quest to find the spirit of the Silk Road. A man named Kurbam sat in the passenger's seat of my Jeep, instructing me in Turkmen to drive off the dirt road bordering a cotton field and into a line of ruts in the sand. Dovelet had suggested that we visit the ancient ruins of Margush, which pre-dated the cities of Merv. Kurbam was the brother of a friend of Dovelet's first uncle; a convoluted but typical familial arrangement that I had come to accept in Turkmenistan. Everything seemed to be done through a network of personal and family relationships.

The day before, Dovelet and I had returned to Uncle Murdan's house to arrange for a guide. My visit coincided with the Muslim holiday of Eid, known in Turkmenistan as Kurban Bairam. The Eid commemorated Abraham's willingness to sacrifice his son Ismail to show his dedication to God. Abraham had been permitted to kill a sheep in his place. It had the same holiday feel as the American Thanksgiving. Families come together, they eat a lot of food and, instead of a turkey, they slaughter a sheep. They have to eat the whole thing in one day or it leaves a kind of bad spirit in the household. All the villages erected giant swings that looked like a primitive ride devised for a county fair. Custom said that one should swing on these contraptions to erase one's sins. Outside Uncle Murdan's house, a dozen children were laughing as they rode the neighborhood's festival swing.

Dovelet showed me through a doorway through a high wall and into a rear courtyard with grape ivy, pear, and pomegranate trees. We met the Uncle Murdan's five teenage daughters plus three more female cousins. The young girls consorted easily and naturally with each other. They sat on a bench swing together under a courtyard trellis or did chores like cooking or sweeping as if conjoined. Each girl wore a soft green, full-length dress in observance of the Turkmen festival. In the back of the courtyard hung a sheep carcass by the hind legs, skinned from the loins to the hips—a contrast in color and texture, half matted black wool and half-smooth pink flesh. A male cousin working on it introduced himself as the "murderer" of the sheep. The slaughter had to be conducted according to prescribed Islamic custom.

Uncle Murdan was expected home momentarily, and we were seated on the floor of a parlor covered with tribal rugs and a plastic picnic mat. The daughters served us green tea, local apricots, raisins, and candies. When not serving us, the young women sat together in a line, like beautiful little birds perched on a branch, all quietly crouched against the wall in the background without saying anything. Every so often one of the sisters would gently rise up and go tend to some unseen chore, and another would come in and sit down in her place. Their round faces with dark features and long dark hair worn up on the head were all variations on a similar theme of beauty. The family resemblances were clear, and the combination of sisters created a mosaic that was almost hypnotic.

While I could reasonably guess that a typical teenage American girl might be thinking of Britney Spears or the latest fashions, I had no idea what thoughts these Turkmen girls might have had. The daughters were to be seen and not heard. Their silence was part of their beauty, giving them a sense of grace and mystery. If they had been chattering away, their beauty might have dissipated.

Uncle Murdan came in the door with his wife to find their household running smoothly. In contrast to her many daughters, the mother assumed the stature of an authority figure. As she gave instructions to her husband, I noticed her muscular forearms that represented years of hard work raising her family. Dovelet had said it was possible that she could become the next chief of the clan when the presiding family matriarch—the same one that Eileen and I met on our last trip—passed on.

Dovelet talked to Uncle Murdan about our plan. The arrangements were made. Murdan would meet us tomorrow to introduce Kurban, and we would drive to the ruins of Margush.

* * *

We met Kurban at his home in the desolate cotton fields north of Mary. Introduced in the usual Turkmen way with a double-handed clasp, and the greeting of "Salaam," his response was impassive while simultaneously conveying a sense of superiority. I found this puzzling. I wondered how this man, in his barren surroundings, could convey such a strong sense of pride. It only occurred to me later that, like Dovelet, he was understandably proud because he was tied to a culture thousands of years old, the remains of which were here in his backyard.

Once off-road, Kurbam navigated through a series of gestures instructing me to drive into dry streambeds, flat desert, over sand dunes, and around mud pits. I hoped my Jeep would perform like advertised in those commercials showing robust off-road, go-anywhere-do-anything adventure. The steering wheel felt mushy in my hands as if I was driving on under-inflated tires. All that I could remember about four-wheel driving was: *keep the tires moving.*

Every so often the absurdity of my situation would occur to me. I was in the company of three Turkmen, dependent on one man—Dovelet—to translate, while driving through unmarked desert wasteland. I realized that no one at the Embassy knew exactly where I was. Plus, I had violated the first rule of desert travel: Always travel with at least three vehicles in your caravan. If one got stuck the second could pull the first out and the third could go for help. Eileen, who knew the dangers of desert driving from experience in the Middle East, would not have been happy had she known of my stupidity.

Keep the tires moving.

I tugged the steering wheel right and left through heavy sand to keep the wheels from rutting into the sand.

After an hour, we were moving through a featureless horizon. The sound of the in-line six cylinders labored in and out of small sand dunes mixed with the occasional scratch of thorny shrubs against the Jeep's skid plates.

Keep the tires moving.

At the end of the two hours, we crested a small ridge overlooking what seemed like a giant maze of mud walls. This was the foundation of the ancient city of Margush spread out before my wheels.

Margush had only been discovered in the early 1980's,

a recent find in archeological terms. Excavation had been slow, but initial artifacts created an extraordinary debate among archeologists and historians. Before Margush, the four oldest centers of the world's civilizations known were Mesopotamia, Egypt, India and China. Due to the research at this site, it was suggested that there was a possible fifth center—Margush. Many of the finds here dated as far back as 3rd millennium BC.

This set of ruins was located in the same delta of the Murgap River as Merv but predated it by at least some six hundred years, or 1,200 years before Christ. The settlement had been a combination fortress, palace, and a miniature city described by Soviet archeologists as a "gala."

We walked the revealed foundation, tracing where the walls of interconnected palace rooms would have been. Broken segments of pipes protruded from the floor showing advanced indoor plumbing, and there was even a series of slots used as an air conditioning system. Rooms for cooking were located near the outside walls of the palace.

The religion of the pre-Islamic inhabitants had emphasized funeral rituals. There were special rooms for washing bodies to be prepared for burial.

Shards of pottery lay all over the ground. Some had been left where they had been uncovered. The saddest items were shards of small pots interspersed with small bones—I recognized femurs and tibias. These were the remains of children. Parents would put the body of a dead child out in the desert to be consumed by scavengers down to the bone. From ancient times, people of central Asia had passed on their dead through "sky burials." Pre-Islamic Turkmen worshiped the heavens and prayed to the sky god *Tengri*. Afterwards, the bones would be placed in small clay pots and preserved. Other collections of pottery had been placed in orderly heaps around the outside of the excavation.

"When Merv died so did Margush," Kurbam explained.

His sparse comments translated through Dovelet left more questions than answers.

"This place was destroyed by fire and abandoned," Kurbam said as if it had happened last week. He pointed to what looked like charred sections of foundation. "Peasants and shepherds later lived here."

I examined some of the pottery. Almost none of it was decorated. I saw one rim section with the raised emblem of a bird but kept hoping I might find a fully intact water jug with a picture of Alexander the Great driving a chariot into battle or a bearded Greek throwing a discus.

Kurbam walked on top of the mud walls looking down into the foundation. This was not a good idea, as they easily crumbled. Dovelet encouraged me to climb up to a small mound of excavated dirt to get a better view of the site and to take a picture. Unfortunately, Turkmenistan's most valuable archeological ruins were not protected, and visitors like us could pretty much walk around the site without the watchful eye of any custodian. I jumped up on the wall of one of the palace rooms, and it crumbled and gave way. I fell about ten feet, driving my head into the dirt. I lay stunned, face down on the earthen floor of what had been a hallway in the ancient palace of Margush. An earthy, sandy smell of Central Asian soil held my attention. All I could see were the dirt walls of the narrow hallway. It was as if I were in an open grave. I sat up to brush the clumps of dirt matted in my hair. I heard Dovelet calling my name. My first thought was: "I've just destroyed the link to the fifth ancient civilization"

* * *

That night we were invited to Dovelet's father-in-law's for the feast of Kurban Bairam. Men and women sat on the floor in separate rooms. The conversation was conducted in Turkmen, so I could not make use of my meager Russian skills.

More food was brought out than a hungry adult could have possibly consumed. Large bowls of soup were filled with potatoes and every part of a sheep imaginable. I carefully spooned out my soup, taking care not to mistake an eyeball for a potato. I had heard stories that the foreigner was considered the guest of honor and should be offered the sheep's head. This did not happen. Young boys brought out heaping plates of *plov* dripping with sheep fat.

"*Plov* is best eaten with the hands," Dovelet advised me. "If you want to be a real Turkmen you must do this."

According to Dovelet, there was something about the natural human oils in the fingers that enhanced the *plov*. Still, my hosts were familiar with Western practices, and a fork was placed before me. During the parade of courses, I began to feel like a bloated sheep myself. Perhaps the spirit of the animal was to be transferred to its human consumers. I eased back on the pillow that was provided for the post-meal coma. Most of the questions that other guests directed at me concerned yesterday's Olympic hockey match between the Russians and the U.S. The Turkmen were deeply troubled by the defeat. Here we were, seemingly cut off from current news, yet my hosts were well informed on this point. I was trying to grasp how there could be any hockey fans in a desert country without a single ice rink. Maybe there was a little bit of "Soviet Man" left in them.

The evening's entertainment came from someone Dovelet called "grandfather" even though he was more like a great uncle. He wore his white beard in the distinctive Turkmen style, without a mustache, and his face was the color and texture of a walnut shell.

Grandfather played the dutar; it had a plaintive, almost unmelodic sound but was evocative and lonely in the way an American cowboy might sound strumming a weather-beaten guitar around a campfire. He played for our group that included Dovelet's three-year-old son. The old man's playing entranced the boy, who normally had the energy of the herd of wild Tekke horses. At one moment, Dovelet told his young son to gently clamp down on the neck of the dutar with his teeth while the grandfather strummed.

"It is Turkmen folklore that this will put Turkmen music in his brain forever," said Dovelet.

Grandfather then handed Yousef the instrument. Given his level of energy, I thought he would wildly flail at it, but instead the three-year-old strummed it in a controlled, skillful way.

At midnight, Dovelet gathered his family to return home. Grandfather insisted we stay, pointing to me in particular. This was the other side of the Turkmen Clan. While initially suspicious of outsiders, once they got to know you, Turkmen pressed their hospitality almost to the point that you felt they wanted you to join their clan. In 1881, Edmund O'Donovan, a special correspondent to the London *Daily News*, was taken as a prisoner by the Merv Tekkes. At first, the tribe debated whether or not to cut his throat. His life was spared, but he continued to be held against his will. All his actions were the subject of great curiosity, especially when he wrote in his journal. After several months of this, he was offered an honorary position of leadership of the tribe. Babies were even named after him because it was the custom among the Merv Tekkes to give newborns the name of any distinguished visitor who happened to be traveling through at the time of their birth. (Once when our Ambassador was visiting the nearby town of Bairam Aly, a man of the village informed us that he had just named his newborn, "Ambassador.") Despite the "honor," O'Donovan found his host's "power to inflict annoyance and their obtuseness to any sense of delicacy, [made] them a most undesirable race to live among." He eventually gained his freedom and never wanted to return.

That night I slept easily on the futon-like mats of Dovelet's family home. My stomach was full of *plov* and mutton and my head with Turkmen music.

* * *

As I left Merv the next morning, I still felt no connection between the modern tribal descendants and Merv's inhabitants of a thousand years ago. They were, I had come to understand, part of an ever-changing kaleidoscope of tribal groups migrating and warring over the expanse of Central Asia.

Then, while packing the Jeep to leave Merv for the last time, Dovelet gave me a Turkmen carpet, hand-woven by his sister-in-law with the design of the traditional Tekke *gul*. Woven into the intricate border of crimson hues were our two family names followed by the words "Friendship Carpet."

The Turkmen had been a rug-weaving people who had taken their craft with them from the cold steppes of central Asia to the fabled city of Merv. Their skill had survived the Mongols and the Russians, and their carpets had been exported over the Silk Road from China to Europe and the Middle East. The wool came from the same hearty breed of sheep that lived in the open spaces, and the knots had been tied with the same technique to form the same patterns. Now, in those same knots, used centuries ago, our names were literally tied together with the symbol of the Tekke tribe. The carpet was the link to the Turkmen past.

JOURNEY 5

In the Footsteps of Alexander

We are linked by blood, and blood is memory without language.
                                                    --Joyce Carol Oates

Larry steered the Suburban off the main road toward the fog-shrouded Kopet Dag Mountains. The secondary road, a strip of crumbled asphalt, pointed dead south in a straight line. Six miles more, and the asphalt deteriorated into a passable gravel track following the contours of a streambed. The gravel dissipated, leaving only a dirt trail that took hold in a series of switchbacks and hairpins. Shallow cloud banks pooled in corners of the landscape, like some sort of primordial residue. The crude terrain evoked something prehistoric, almost as if around the next corner we would meet a lost group of Neanderthals who have just discovered fire and stone tools.

After half an hour of white knuckle driving, I began to wonder whether it was wise to bring Eileen and Charlotte. Eileen worried. I was putting our small family at risk on the slippery mountain roads.

We were looking for the enigmatic Nokhur people who

inhabited several villages in the Kopet Dag. With their blue eyes and Mediterranean features, they were said by the Turkmen to be descendants of Alexander the Great.

* * *

A couple months after our arrival, Larry introduced Eileen and me to Serdar, a Turkmen friend of his who had worked with several international development programs. Serdar learned of Eileen's interest in anthropology and asked if we wanted to make a trip with Larry to visit the Nokhur region. Serdar volunteered to serve as a guide to find the Nokhur's home in the Kopet Dag.

"Sounds great," I said, not really thinking of what was involved. I was more excited by the idea of the adventure. The Nohkur were an isolated tribe in an isolated country. After the artificial world of Ashgabat, I was anxious to see the other face of Turkmenistan.

Despite over seventy years of Soviet rule, Turkmenistan is still a tribal society just below the surface. Of the 140 tribes and sub-tribes, the Nokhur were considered among the most closed and incongruous of them. Major tribes, like the Tekke and Yomut, dominated the country's politics and are well known for their horses, as well as centuries-old weaving traditions that have produced some of the world's most beautiful textiles by which the Turkmen are known. The Nokhur, on the other hand, do not make carpets—a significant distinction in this textile-centered society. They are rarely represented in the government, and government representatives are virtually non-existent in the Nokhur villages. At the time of our visit, the region's *hakeem* had not set foot in the village in the two years since he had been appointed.

That gray January morning, as Larry drove at a crawl along the mountain road, Serdar explained in his excellent English, "The Nokhur claim a unique ancestry to Alexander the Great and his generals. Some of them have blue eyes and aquiline noses that are different than the features of most of the rest of the Turkmen."

The northern limit of Alexander's Empire had run along the geographic boundary between the foothills of the Kopet Dag and the sands of the Kara Kum—approximately where we turned off the main road. In 330 BC, Alexander defeated the Parthians and began a campaign of pacification, founding cites that became an unusual mixture of Greek and local influences in architecture, religion, language, and culture. He built seven towns in what is now Turkmenistan. He marched his forces eastward, staying within the shadows of the mountains, and then arced north to build the legendary walled city of Merv at the Margiana Oasis.

Along the way, Alexander left officers to administer his newly acquired territories and to marry daughters of the local tribal chiefs. Alexander himself later married Princess Roxanna, daughter of the fiercest of the Bactrian Chiefs, in what is now neighboring Afghanistan. The Nohkur, Serdar said, claimed part of this Greek legacy.

* * *

After another hour of fogbound travel, the first sign of civilization appeared as the outline of a mud walled house perched on the rocky bluffs above the road. We found the village of Nohkur, for which we spent half the day searching. The houses, constructed of rough, dry, mud wall construction, looked like a cross between a medieval Middle East town and a Hopi pueblo village.

The chickens, cows, and goats of Nokhur roamed the dirt main street oblivious to the Suburban. Boys, not older than six or seven, tended horned cows in the middle of the street. They looked at us with grim-faced expressions of disapproval closer to what one might expect of wizened old farmers glowering at joy-riding city slickers than normally curious, carefree, young boys.

Only minutes into the village center and we had become the Saturday afternoon spectacle for a gallery of men in woolly hats. The Suburban, about the size of a small power-boat, mired itself in a slippery cesspool of mud, sewage, and debris. Rain had fallen on the village for the last two days. Larry and I got out, carefully studying the mess. Shards of sharp, rusty machine fragments hidden in the quagmire could easily have punctured our tires.

Serdar took advantage of our involuntary stop, stepped out of the truck and approached the friendliest-looking spectator. The man gave a wan smile from behind a face of sandstone skin, hooked nose, and blue eyes. In his early thirties, he wore a black double-breasted coat and mud-speckled pants. He spoke to Serdar in Turkmen but talked to the other villagers in a dialect Serdar could not understand. Serdar thought it an older version of Turkmen but could not be sure. The Nokhur's blue eyes and Mediterranean features seemed completely out of place in a country of brown eyes and Asiatic features.

When Serdar assured him we were harmless, Blue Eyes asked if we were interested in "the sacred tree."

During their ten-minute conversation, I worked to wedge scraps of wood under the rear tires to gain traction. I had visions of the giant Suburban being sucked into the sludge like a dinosaur being entrapped in the La Brea Tar Pits, only to be discovered millions of years later by perplexed scientists. Before my imagination worked further, Larry maneuvered the four-wheel drive in reverse gear to gain enough traction on the wood scraps to free us from the cesspool. Larry parked on the most stable patch of mud available.

Blue Eyes led us along the street around generous deposits of cow dung. I hoisted my daughter on my shoulders and picked my steps as carefully as if I were walking through a minefield. A stream that ran through the main street also served as the town's sewer system. Road, stream, and sewer intermingled and were indistinguishable at points. The freezing-point temperatures muted what would have otherwise made an incredible smell.

Along the street, homeowners marked their yards with fences constructed of the crudest piles of rocks, sticks and vines. Houses of the more prosperous were detached, low rambling structures, set back from the road and tucked against hillsides.

We stepped off the street and up a short rise of stone steps to the porch of a home. The porch was decorated with wooden columns hand-carved into scrolled rough "Doric" style supports at the top. Through Serdar's translation, Blue Eyes claimed that such columns were unique to his tribe. This simple flourish made the house seem like the Acropolis of Nokhur.

The holy tree was in a courtyard, behind a collapsing building whose walls were so crumbled that the bricks could easily have been pulled out by hand. It was an ancient oak with the circumference of a small grain silo but only 50 feet in height—much shorter than its massive trunk suggested. It had been hollowed out by rot, yet the branches were still filled with life. There was an opening at the base in the shape of an inverted "V" about three and a half feet high—the right size for a troll. Blue Eyes gestured that we should step inside.

Each of us took a turn stooping to enter through the opening. Stepping inside, it was possible to stand up in the darkness. The sounds of breathing or talking were absorbed by the interior walls. It was like standing in a dark, soundproof booth. The tree was hollow all the way to the top so looking up to a small circle of gray sky was like looking up the length of a smokestack. Charlotte was not the least bit afraid. When she stepped inside with my wife, her two-year-old instincts told her to call out of the top like it was a giant megaphone.

How the tree gained holy status was not clear. Our guide could offer no specifics. It was not unusual in Turkmenistan for trees to be sacred. Co-existing with Turkmen Islam are older religious beliefs to which pilgrimage to holy shrines, burial sites of folk heroes and ancestors are central. Associated with these holy sites are usually trees and springs. The word Nokhur itself was borrowed by Persians from Arabic and translated as "river" or "the stream way."

Nokhur religious practices were a concoction of asceticism—Nokhur weddings have no dancing or alcohol—and ancient animist practices cloaked under a veneer of popular Islam. Local shrines and sacred natural sites were very important to the Nokhur, despite Soviet attempts to eradicate religion. The best examples of this were in the rural places like Nokhur.

Like at other holy sites in Turkmenistan, a cemetery was situated nearby, almost as if the site emanated a sacred power that would offer a blessing to the dead. The graves were marked with a ram's skull mounted on heavy sticks. The skull's corkscrew horns were forever frozen at its growth in mid-spiral. This was another symbol of the Nokhur's pre-Islamic practices. But why a ram's skull? The significance baffled even one Ashgabat academic from Turkmen State University who had studied the Nokhur for years.

From our vantage point in the graveyard, we could see a group of four men in coarse, black, wool *tilpek* hats sitting on a bench. They could have been swapping the latest news. A group of women with head coverings of small ornamental "coats" of rough, red silk walked single file, giving them the appearance of colorful nuns marching in solemn procession through a medieval town.

Nokhur men and women segregate their activities almost

as strictly as the Shakers do. Women, even grandmothers, wear the stylized "coats" as head coverings. Normally, Turkmen brides would wear these coverings for the first forty days after their wedding. The Nokhur women even covered their heads while washing clothes in streambeds or working in their gardens. Their long, coffee-colored hair was braided into three long strands, unlike the traditional Turkmen style of two. Serdar had no explanation for the three braids except to point out that it was another idiosyncrasy of the Nokhur.

We were only 100 miles west of Turkmenistan's capital city where President Niyazov's billboard-sized portrait appeared everywhere, and the government buildings had been remade with white marble facades. Nearly every town and village I had seen posted the president's likeness somewhere. Nokhur, however, had no portraits and no white-marbled buildings. Nokhur's isolation has preserved many of the old folkways, kept out change and given them a closer connection to their tribal roots than their Turkmen cousins in the cities. Considered clannish, odd and even backward by other Turkmen, their rough American equivalent might be the mountain people of Appalachia.

We clamored down from the graveyard and Serdar and I found the only statue in town—a small bust of a famous Turkmen general on a pedestal. The general had been the last of the Central Asians to be conquered by the Russians. Serdar said that this general had been one of the Turkmen commanders who had held out the longest against the Russian takeover in the 1880's.

We wanted to see beyond the village. Our party took turns lightly clasping hands with Blue Eyes. I said "Thagbol" ("Thank-you"), one of the few Turkmen words I knew, and hoped he understood my novice pronunciation.

Larry drove us south and further up the dirt track. Breaking above the clouds into a harsh, ice-blue, windswept sky, the Suburban felt like an airplane climbing out of a cloudbank into the sunshine. At the edge of an overhang, we looked down on the valley from where we'd just come. Somewhere in the drifting cloudbanks below was Nokhur. Nearby was an abandoned shepherd's hut, with a five-star scenic view. Its occupant must have been driven off by loneliness or the blasts of freezing wind. The high plateau and rugged snow peaks in the distance reminded my wife more of the Hindu Kush than of anything we had seen in Turkmenistan.

We attempted to picnic in the shelter of some boulders to shield ourselves from the gale. Larry and I ate outside like savages, standing, chomping on cold chicken legs while moving around to keep warm. To a passerby, we might have appeared to be natives dancing an unrhythmic, tribal jig. Eileen, Charlotte, and Serdar ate in the Suburban.

Minutes after our impromptu lunch began, a battered dull green Soviet-era army jeep pulled up behind the Suburban and a man with the now familiar beaked nose, wearing an English style "mac" stepped out. He asked Serdar if we knew that we were close to the Iranian border and if we had a permit to travel in this border region. I wondered whether he was a plainclothes KNB officer (Turkmenistan's own version of the Soviet KGB), a border guard, or just a concerned passing motorist. He had an intelligent, knowing face. When he saw our two-year-old daughter in the car, his suspicion dissipated. In his next sentence, he invited us to his home for tea. Looking at a wall of dark gray clouds filling the sky behind him, we made excuses not to accept his invitation: we did not have time and were low on gas. He hesitated and then got back in his jeep and drove down the mountain. We drove south another few miles over a bare scratch of road past a desultory chicken farm on top of a high plain. A man pushing a wheelbarrow stopped his work to stare at the Suburban. Even at a distance, it was possible to see how his gaze fixed on the progress of our vehicle.

The road broke into multiple forks. With the storm clouds growing closer and knowing that our daylight was limited to a few hours, we turned around and drove back down the mountain into the clouds.

At the edge of the village, the fog thickened to the point that we had to stop while Serdar ran ahead to peer into the whiteness. Larry wanted some warning whether we were still on the road or about to plunge over a precipice into one of the desolate rock gorges below. He slowed to a creep to follow Serdar's hand signals. At times the trail seemed to disappear. The worst sections were the steep downhill grades. When we reached the straight roads of the desert floor of the Kara Kum, it was a pleasure to drive under the drizzle and gray cloud cover.

On the drive home toward the white-marbled buildings of Ashgabat, I wondered whether the Nokhur were truly the sons of Alexander. What I saw were Mediterranean features, not the appearance of the average Turkmen, and architectural similarities to the ancient Greeks. The Nokhur, for their part, may believe the stories of the regal Greek lineage. If nothing else, they carry themselves with an air of independence, as though they are different from their desert countrymen. The power of Alexander's Nokhur legacy—true or not—may have given this community the strength to survive as a small, independent tribe.

Since Alexander's time, the Nokhur had been out of history's way. They lived off the map in a country that was off the map for the rest of the world. From what we saw up in the Kopet Dag, this was how the Nokhur preferred it.

* * *

The Nokhur were a living connection to the past. Around Ashgabat there were no living connections, only crumbling ruins. Through our friendship with Serdar, he continued to guide us to other links to the time of Alexander and the Parthians.

On another Saturday afternoon, Serdar directed us about nine miles west of Ashgabat to a collection of ancient ruins on an elevated plain. This was old Nisa that once was the royal seat of power for Parthians around the time of Christ. The Parthians had wrested power from the military descendants of Alexander's empire, the Selucids. Their empire covered Iran and southern Turkmenistan and stretched all the way to Iraq and Syria. The Parthians became the middle power between Rome and China. When we pulled our Jeep up to the gates of the once mighty fortress, it was now only guarded by an old man in a *tilpek*. He appeared from a small hut and, by force of his intense stare, wordlessly charged 20,000 Manat (about one dollar) to enter.

Nisa's location on a set of hills made it a natural site for a fortress. I could look east at desert and mountains. The Parthian Generals would have had a clear view of enemies coming from any direction. Far off in the distance, the needle of the Ninth Anniversary monument was a small spike on the horizon. Nisa would have been a citadel of royal palaces and passages. The remains had thick fortress walls. Most of it had been reconstructed, a common practice in Soviet archeology.

The Parthian Empire created a network of roads that stretched eastward in shadow of the Kopet Dag. The network followed the natural divide of the land, paralleling the mountains and then continuing to Mary. The path was marked by settlements and signal posts for rapid communications. Modern Turkmenistan's two-lane asphalt road to Mary followed the same route that the Parthians used.

* * *

Seven miles east of Ashgabat was the mysterious site of

Anau. There had once been a town here known as "Bagabad" to Alexander, the Parthians, and later Silk Road travelers. The site was considered sacred. During the rule of Timurlane, it was famous for its mosque that was said to rival those of Bukhara and Samarkand, with two domes, a minaret, and a tiled mosaic above the main entrance. Bagabad's buildings were left neglected, and its population shrank, leaving only the mosque that was flattened by the devastating earthquake of 1948.

On a windblown Saturday, Serdar navigated our drive to Anau. It was half a mile off the main road leading out of Ashgabat, but we never would have noticed it as anything other than a low mound of dirt. We drove on a path through a cotton field and pulled in behind a dirt hill. We climbed the hill to find remains of the mosque, still with columns, and walls with their blue-tiled mosaics. Some tiles lay on the ground, suitable for archeologists to study without any digging required. Most impressive was a partial mosque dome still intact.

We overlooked a small plain that stretched to the Kopet Dag Mountains. The wind gusted over the rubble, enhancing the feeling of desolation. Three Turkmen Alabai dogs, the size of Great Danes and accompanied by a tabby cat, chaperoned us around the site. The dogs did not rush up to us or bark but were strangely quiet, considering we were strangers on their territory. They quietly followed us at a distance as we walked the ruins.

A father and mother with their three-year-old boy were the only other people there. The boy was unable to walk, and they believed that circling certain holy stones on the site would cure his paralysis. There was a well-worn dirt path around the sacred marker.

We noticed hundreds of bricks and stones arranged like tiny houses. There were also tiny replicas of cradles, made of scraps of cloth, rattles, and bits of children's clothing. Serdar quietly explained that these were fertility offerings.

Anau may have been older than any site in Turkmenistan. Some archeologists have shown that there were signs of a settlement at this location as far back as the late Stone Age, around the 4th Millenium BC. The ancient finds were first studied by an American archeologist in 1904, and then further studied by Dr. Fred Heibert of the University of Pennsylvania months before our visit. Dr. Heibert had found a stone seal in a complex of buildings south of the mosque. The seal showed a form of writing that stumped the world's leading experts. The seal dated hundreds of years before the Chinese system of writing had come into being. The small seal meant that an independent civilization had once flourished there. Now, nothing was left but a dirt mound and the wreckage of a mosque.

* * *

On a Sunday, we continued to follow the path of the Parthians but this time on our own. We traveled in a two-truck caravan with an Embassy colleague and his family to a site about 65 miles east of Ashgabat called Abiwerd. Our route carried us southeast, parallel to the Kopet Dag on our right. As we left Ashgabat's city limits, the road marked a natural boundary on the land. To the right, the land was green and cultivated all the way to the Kopet Dag's foothills. To the left, the land ran flat and arid to the horizon. The effect was forbidding—like looking out onto an ocean knowing a great storm was raging over the horizon. Here, we were looking at the edge of a great barren desert that stretched for hundreds of miles. Our path followed a route thousands of years old that linked ancient settlements at the base of the mountains, settlements that predated the Silk Road.

Along the route, often in the middle of nowhere, were bus shelters made out of a couple of poles with a concrete slab roof, offering minimal cover to a hard slat bench. They looked like stage sets for a French existentialist play. Periodically people would be waiting; men in the squatting position, women bundled up in scarves and coats carrying cheap laminated plaid bags known throughout Central Asia as "babushka bags." The two-lane road was unlined, uneven and narrow. Farm roads in Ohio would feel like the Autobahn by comparison. My Embassy colleague drove his Land Cruiser at speeds approaching 80 mph on the uneven blacktop roads. The Chevy Suburban, which already handled like a dirigible, was made even more unwieldy by the bumps and dips.

Only a simple sign marked the ruins of Abiwerd. The sign read in Turkmen that this was an administrative center for the Parthian civilization. The settlement was outlined by two large mounds of earth that would have been the walls of a fortress guarding the city. The remaining walls of the town looked like they had been melted down to heights of three to five feet high. Doorways and bottoms of window frames were all that was left. The structures were made of mud bricks. A dry riverbed ringed part of the settlement. The ground was covered with mixed pottery shards, soda cans, and bits of modern glass bottles, some with very colorful scraps of designs and brown glazes. No excavation had been done. I could not tell if I was looking at pieces that were ten years old or a thousand. Over the first mound we could see another cluster of ruins about a quarter mile away. Beyond this second settlement was a double-domed Muslim mausoleum still in use. Eileen and I started to hike toward the mausoleum but quickly give up after realizing that it was at least a couple miles away.

Back at our vehicles, two men wearing *tilpek* hats pulled up in a white Lada. One identified himself as a local archeologist, the other a photographer. They showed us an area they said they had recently started excavating. It covered about 20 square feet of an embankment. Sitting in the dig was a three-foot tall, dull-clay colored urn. It had been pieced together from several large fragments. Pottery shards were piled around the dirt above it. About 50 feet along the embankment was a second excavation project. This one showed clay pipe fittings. This had been the plumbing system. The men had only broken the surface of these two small areas with not much more than a spade and their bare hands. Eileen felt that they did not know the first thing about archeology and thought they were KNB sent to keep watch on us.

Across the road was an earthen mound about the size of a high school football stadium. These had been built as signaling stations by Alexander the Great's army, and later improved upon by the Parthians. The mounds ran in a line from Mary to Nisa. Built within sighting distance of each other, signalers used mirrors in the desert sun to transmit messages, allowing communications to travel the hundreds of miles in half a day. The irony was that near every signaling mound was a microwave-repeating tower for cell phone transmissions. Thousands of years passed, but the signal towers continued.

Driving back to Ashgabat, the sun was off our left shoulder, perched at the top of the mountain line. From that position, it cast a shadow that neatly paralleled the road. Darkness had eclipsed the south side of the road while warm sunlight still bathed the desert side on the north. In a few minutes, the line of shadows moved over the road completely, and we watched the sunlight recede into the desert.

JOURNEY 6

Two Hours Beyond the End of the Earth

If you reject the food, ignore the customs, fear the religion and avoid the people, you might better stay home.

--James Michener

In February, I visited the end of the earth. I was sent on a trip to monitor an American-funded water treatment facility in a rural area of the northern province of Dashoguz. Turkmenistan's infant mortality was the highest in Central Asia in part because large segments of the population suffered from waterborne diseases. The water plant provided clean drinking water to the most affected areas, which happened to be remote agricultural communities.

If *Lonely Planet* was right about Ashgabat, Dashoguz had to be the end of the earth. My map showed that the town was located between the deserts of Turkmenistan and Uzbekistan. The remoteness was no matter to the Turkmen government authorities. They still considered it a restricted border zone. I needed a special travel permit to visit. Turkmenistan's President had announced plans to build a fence along its border with Uzbekistan and Kazakhstan to keep out "dishonest people."

The morning I left for the airport, snow covered the Kopet Dag, making them look like giant lumps of dough sprinkled with powdered sugar. The peaks were obscured by clouds of cold mist. The mountains presented an unpleasant omen.

At the empty ticket counter, I joined a hopeful mob waiting to have their tickets validated. Half an hour passed. Nothing. Then a formidable ethnic Russian ticket agent appeared. Under a shock of chemically assisted white-blond hair, she had the physique of a former body-builder and the bearing of a surly Hell's Angel. The mob reacted with all the decorum of a stage-side crowd at a Madison Square Garden rock concert. Fur hats and scarved heads all pushed forward in a melee thrusting tickets toward the ticket agent from two or three rows back. Those few who had their tickets validated battled their way out of the crowd as people tried to occupy their space even before they vacated.

After about eight or nine customers had been served, there was a sharp, huffy exchange between a Turkmen woman and the ticket agent. The ticket agent stormed away from her post and disappeared behind a door. While I did not understand enough Russian to know exactly what had been said, it was clear that the ticket agent was not coming back. No announcement was made on what to expect next. I went to the gate to show my ticket but was made to understand, more by body language than through my knowledge of Russian, that the flight was not boarding and that I should turn around and go home. Not accepting this, I walked over to the empty lounge reserved for international flights. They helped me board after paying a "customer service fee." I was the last one to board the Soviet Yak-40, workhorse of the Turkmen Air fleet. Mysteriously, the flight was full with the same folks who had led the assault on the ticket counter. Now they all sat passively in their seats.

During the hour-long flight, we flew over the heart of the

Kara Kum Desert. Though the name meant "black sand," it looked more like a pair of deeply wrinkled khaki pants. Dashouz had been the name during Soviet times, which literally translated in Turkmen as "stone reservoir." Recently the President had changed the name slightly to Dashoguz. This was said to reflect the proper spelling and true historical significance of the place, meaning "place of the far Oghuz." The Oghuz had been the original Turkmen tribe that led to the 140 tribes and sub-tribes that made up Turkmenistan today. Dashoguz was home to a branch of the Yomut tribe, one of the most powerful tribes, second only to the Tekke.

Looking down at the blankness of the Kara Kum, I tried to imagine what I would find at the end of the earth. I pictured a near void, containing a lone camel chewing its cud, a cast-off spare tire and a brown plastic grocery bag wafting across the landscape like a tumble weed in an unrelenting wind. The reality was different. As we approached for landing, I could see stretches of dusty cotton fields with unlined irrigation trenches and drab concrete block buildings the same color as the sandy brown fields. It looked like a suitable place to exile political prisoners.

At Dashoguz Airport I was pulled aside by border security officials who studied my passport and travel permits. At the town's only official guesthouse my travel documents were rechecked. That evening, I decided to call Eileen to find out about her day and let her know I arrived safely. She had been scheduled to observe the trial of a local man who was being evicted from his home for meeting with a small group of Turkmen Baptists. The trial had been part of the government's systematic persecution of Protestants; harassing, arresting and torturing citizens who attempted to form congregations that had not been state sanctioned. Activities of all but the state-controlled Sunni Muslim and Russian Orthodox faiths were essentially outlawed. The year before,

Government bulldozers attempted to level a building used as a church. I knew Turkmen who feared arrest by the Secret Police simply for having a Bible in their possession.

I could not just pick up the phone and call the outside world. I had to "order" a phone call. The process started with a confusing ten-minute exchange with a man who arrived at my door. I believed—but am not sure to this day—that he was a hotel employee. I gave him 40,000 Manat (about $2 at the unofficial exchange rate) to walk to the telephone exchange and call Eileen, who was then supposed to call me back. Twenty minutes later, the plastic phone in my room that looked more like a prop from some parallel universe of the 1950's than the real thing, sputtered a series of distressed buzzing sounds. It was Eileen, still confused by the Russian-speaking man who called. She was on the line long enough for me to shout, "I'm Alive!" The connection went dead.

I fell asleep in a disoriented funk.

* * *

I woke to a slate gray dawn unsure of my surroundings. The bathroom electricity did not work so I conducted my morning ablutions in darkness under a steady trickle of freezing water.

Outside, a fierce, frigid wind chilled my face as if I had been doused with a bucket of ice. I had hired a local driver and an interpreter for my two-hour drive to Turkmenbashi Etrap (an etrap is the equivalent of a U.S. county). The driver was waiting by the curb in an aging Lada. The passenger's door groaned as I opened it to step in.

The driver, Atamurat, was a stoic, serenely confident man wearing a *tilpek*, and like his Lada, it was hard to gauge his age. He might have been anywhere between his late twenties or early forties. I caught a glint of life to Attamurat's brown eyes and guessed perhaps thirty-five. Maral was my interpreter. She was an English teacher at the local elementary school and spoke with a slight British accent. She immediately apologized for her poor language abilities. Her English was excellent. Both grew up in the countryside around Dashoguz.

As we drove northeast, out of town, the Soviet-style cement block apartment buildings quickly ebbed from view, giving way to barren countryside. It was not so much a void as a half-finished landscape. Rudimentary human settlements made of sandstone-colored blocks blended with the dusty-brown color of the land. The clumps of houses looked completely forsaken under the gray sky. Shallow trenches, for irrigation or gas pipelines scarred much of the landscape. Mud was everywhere. There were occasional reminders of active human habitation—a lone figure tromping through a muddy field, or a bare light bulb shining from a one-room house. Atamurat and Maral offered conversation about recipes for *plov* as a reassuring contrast to the desolation outside.

Roads, even through villages, were unpaved. The emptiness became more pronounced, broken only by passing fragments of life. An old man in a skullcap and white beard shuffled along the muddy thoroughfares. The driver of an old, squat Soviet-era bus bent down in front of it, straining to start the motor with an iron hand crank. A young woman in heavy robes and a colorful headscarf, wrapped around her head, rode sidesaddle on a motor scooter behind a man—possibly her brother or husband. A gray-brown donkey, led by a six-year-old boy, pulled a two-wheeled wooden cart overloaded with long green stalks of mulberry branches. A small herd of white goats, atop a crude barn lazily ate at the thatched roof, seemingly oblivious to the cold winds.

After two hours, we arrived in the main village of Turkmenbashi Etrap. We were greeted by USAID's local contact, Agajan. He was a stocky fellow with an impassive, ruddy face. My accommodations were at his home, which doubled as a guesthouse. I was his first customer. His daughter served us a filling lunch of hot mutton, rice with sheep fat, and apricots. The daughter piled ridiculous-sized helpings on my plate.

The lunch made me groggy but I was expected to make a courtesy call on the local *hakeem*, to introduce myself and discuss the water distribution program. Agajan drove me in his Yaz, the Soviet Army's answer to the Jeep. During my brief meeting with the *hakeem*, he told me that the local people have begun referring to the clean drinking water as "American water." Other communities had seen their success and the *hakeem* wanted like additional assistance to build more water treatment plants. He seemed to think I had a bag of money and could hand over what he needed if only I agreed. I had to convince him that I was only here to monitor how well American aid dollars were being spent.

Agajan seemed to know what was expected next. We drove an hour over the worst roads in the country to an elementary school in the outlying settlement of Altekke, where clearly they were waiting for "the American." An anxious principal escorted me to a room with the entire student body and faculty to watch young children perform a skit about water and sanitation. The highpoint of the drama unfolded with the demise of one child who clutched his stomach and rolled to the ground, all because he did not wash his hands before eating. The children lived in the community that received the "American Water." It was delivered by tanker trucks and distributed at cisterns strategically located in the neighborhoods.

Following the schoolhouse drama, we drove to inspect one of the neighborhood cisterns. Rationing was done on an honor system and seemed to work. Old men in *tilpeks* and the white Captain Ahab-like beards crowded around to watch me peer into the concrete cistern. One middle-aged man stepped forward and passionately read a poem of his own composition about having clean drinking water. I grew uncomfortable having so much attention directed at me. The only thing I could think of was to call the poet the "Maktumguli of Turkmenbashi Etrap." Maktumguli was Turkmenistan's most famous poet, the Shakespeare of the Turkmen language. It would be like trying to complement an English-language poet by calling him the Bard of Sandusky, Ohio.

That night, Agajan offered me the opportunity to sleep in a yurt set up in the backyard of his house. It was about 15°F outside. I opted for a room inside with a futon-style bed on the floor.

* * *

Morning broke with a rooster's crow from the roof. I had no meetings today. Agajan offered to show me some "old fortresses." Horrible roads required us to start at six a.m. if we were to return before dark. Agajan's Yaz crawled through a network of muddy ruts. After an hour, I realized he had no map. I had no map. I had no idea where we were. My best guess was the northwestern border area with Uzbekistan.

When there appeared to be no road, I saw the outlines of what looked like dirt mounds on the horizon. This was Shamakhi. The name was the only piece of information Agajan could offer. The ruins were a series of forty-foot-high, crenellated battlement walls that once were part of a fortress. From a crease in the gray sky, a swatch of sunlight illuminated one side of the walls. The view to the horizon was of desolation, but I kept trying to remind myself that eight hundred years ago this was a vital center of trading activity to the Turkmen. Shamakhi's last inhabitants either abandoned it or were massacred by the Mongols sometime in the 13th Century. Now, it was nothing but an outpost of melting clay.

Half an hour's drive from Shamaskhi was Devkesken. It was an impressive fortress that sat at the corner of a steep plateau surrounded by a dry moat. Its perimeter was still very much intact and would have been large enough to hold a small town. Agajan did not know its history either, except a partial legend that was hard for me to follow.

With Maral translating, Agajan explained, "a prince from a neighboring kingdom promised the king of this fortress unlimited water in exchange for his daughter's hand in marriage. The prince created the water but later fell into a misunderstanding about whether the daughter was still alive or married to someone else. The prince killed himself. The daughter, who loved the prince, reappeared to find the prince dead and kills herself out of distress."

This was your Turkmen Romeo and Juliet, I wanted to tell him.

"In the end," Agajan said, "the water dried up and the people of the fortress died off."

There was a kernel of truth to this legend. Some historians suggest that, centuries ago, the waters of the Amudarya River that flowed into the Caspian Sea fed this area. Sometime in the 15th or 16th Century, the waters changed course, possibly from an earthquake, flowing away from Devkesken and, instead, to the Aral Sea to the north. Water had been the source of Devkesken's life centuries ago and, after meeting the school children of the Altekke settlement yesterday, it was still as important to their humble settlement.

At one corner of the fortress was a tower that would have been used to watch the dust clouds of approaching caravans or enemy armies. We climbed to the top and looked out over an immense desert plain. Looking down on the void below, I had the feeling of standing at the earth's last outpost. Our small group was buffeted by a wind that had traveled hundreds of miles of desert, unimpeded by forests or mountains. A couple of miles away stood a lone yurt with a few sheep dotted around the back. Beyond was a cluster of sandstone structures, the settlement of Dovkesen.

This was it. This was geographic oblivion. This was as far as I could travel. It might have been what medieval Europeans had in mind when they filled the unknown areas of their maps with dragons and two-headed monsters.

Agajan led us down to walk the inside perimeter of the fortress. Most remarkable was that everything was untouched. No archeological excavation had been done. During the Soviet period this had been a neglected corner of the USSR. The Soviets did not have the interest or resources to fully study it. The fortress was an archeologist's dream. Centuries of unknown history lay under these ruins, but none of it explored. At its center were "dungeons." These were essentially dark pits with vertical sides.

"Bad people would have been thrown or lowered into them as punishment for their misdeeds," Agajan said.

At Dovekesan and Shamakhi, small, domed Muslim shrines had been built in the last hundred years or so. Local Muslims made mini-pilgrimages to the ancient sites where they left small shards of fabric as offerings for curing sickness or for fertility. Some pilgrims would prop two small stones together to mark their visit. My Turkmen companions knelt and said a short prayer in Turkmen with a quick genuflection motion of touching their head and chest. Present-day Turkmen even buried their deceased near the ancient sites, feeling that some sacred power emanated from the ruins to bless the dead. Walking by one of the fortress walls, we saw one grisly reminder of this practice—the partial remains of a human rib cage, still attached to a spinal column. The bones had been exposed through erosion.

* * *

The next morning, I thanked Agajan with a two-handed clasp and a Turkmen Thank-you ("Thagbol") and left the guesthouse with Maral and Atamurat.

On the drive back to Dashoguz, we raced the setting sun to make a brief stop at the ancient city of Koneurgench (or "Old Urgench"). Like much of Central Asia, its date of origin is uncertain. Ceramics from the 5th Century had been unearthed here. It has a complex history, said by legend to have been destroyed and rebuilt seven times. The region had been known as Khorezm which was also the name often applied to the city. In the 13th Century, Ghengis Khan's army massacred the inhabitants, razed most of its stone buildings and dammed its water supply. Within a hundred years, the city recovered to where Ibn Battuta, an Islamic adventure traveler of the Middle Ages, thought it the "grandest and most beautiful and most important city of the Turks." He was amazed with the abundance in the bazaars, its broad streets, and the size of its thriving populace. Khorezm was home to colleges, hospitals, mosques and the overwhelming generosity of its people toward strangers. Two centuries later, Tamerlane, descendant of Ghengis Khan, nicknamed "the Prince of Destruction," enhanced his reputation by destroying the thriving city. The settlement suffered its fatal blow when the Amudarya River changed its flow away from the city, depriving its inhabitants of water.

A sullen young man in his early twenties, dressed in a knock-off Nike warm-up suit, charged me admission to visit the site. He charged a discounted price for Maral. I asked Maral to tell him that I was really Turkmen.

Maral translated that I was Turkmen and wanted a lower price. The young man remained sullen and shook his head no. Maral smiles to be polite. Note to self: No more jokes with the guide. My camera was also charged admission.

The ancient city had been the capital of the ancient kingdom of Khorezm over a thousand years ago. What remained were ruins of a palace, mausoleums, monuments, and Central Asia's tallest existing minaret (a tower used by Muslims to issue the call to prayer), nearly two-hundred feet tall.

Maral translated our guide's rote monotone, "the top of the minaret had a golden tower that was pulled off by Ghengis Khan's men."

I tried to imagine our guide's ancestors fighting for their lives against the Khan's warriors. His lackluster attitude made me think they would have been no match for the Mongol army.

But also, I could not imagine our dour guide's forebears building the sky-blue tiles of the conical dome of the mausoleum dedicated to an Arab ruler known as Sultan Takeshtome. Halfway down the dome, the tiles had been pried off, giving the impression that looters through the ages may not have had ladders long enough to reach to the very top. As we walked the ruins in fading light, Maral covered her head with a scarf.

"This is a very holy place," Maral explained.

Like at Dovekesan, Maral and our Turkmen guide grew quiet and stopped to say short prayers, this time before the above-ground tomb of a princess. Interspersed among the ancient ruins are modern graves—most no older than the 19th Century. Some graves had replicas of ladders lying across the top.

Inside the Sultan Takeshtome mausoleum, someone had started to do rudimentary excavation. Pottery shards sat arranged on one stone mantel of a window. There was too much to try to understand and no time. As the shadow of the minaret grew longer, we were back in Attamurat's Lada, racing to the airport to make the last flight back to Ashgabat.

In the airport's dimly lit granite building, boarding involved another scrum. Even though we were traveling inside the country, I was pulled aside and security officers checked my passport—twice, once by a border guard, the second time by a KNB official. This was like asking a resident of Michigan to have his passports checked before crossing the Ohio state line.

Our flight was another Soviet-made plane, this one a Tu-144, a sizable aircraft suitable for long-distance flights. The interior was a garish 1960's décor of lime green pastel colors loaded with decades of smoke and body odor. Luckily, it was only an hour to Ashgabat. I thought how travel changes perspective. Dashoguz now seemed like Paris. What would Ashgabat feel like? For that matter, what would Paris feel like?

JOURNEY 7

Crossing the Oxus

Even today few Europeans have seen the Oxus,
so remote is its course, and those who have done so
have mostly viewed it from the air when flying.
--Peter Hopkirk, The Great Game

A strong westerly wind gusted all day. The gale had blown for the last three days—strong enough that trees and shrubs on the compound looked permanently bowed to the east, towards Afghanistan. Clouds of dirty brown sand and grit obscured the normally visible Kopet Dag Mountains to the south.

It was the summer of 2001, and Turkmenistan was undergoing its worst drought in decades. The local U.N. office had set up a commission to study the problem. The official government position was that the drought did not exist and that its state-run farms were in the midst of reaping a record cotton crop. The harvest of wheat and cotton reported daily in *Neutral Turkmenistan*, the four-page official newspaper, said so.

Larry had ended his assignment in April and returned to the United States to retire. He had been a mentor and a friend. His departure left me as the only American in Turkmenistan representing USAID. If there was a drought, a first-hand look at the primary source of Turkmenistan's water and the lifeline to its agricultural well-being—the Amudarya River—was needed. USAID had a few small agricultural programs, along with an environmental project, designed to monitor the flow of the Amudarya. Larry had always made a point of traveling the country to see things for himself. With his example in mind, I organized a small team to drive the entire length of the river as it flowed through Turkmen territory.

* * *

The Amudarya starts as a trickle of snowmelt from high in the Pamir Mountains in Tajikistan at the western end of the Tibetan Plateau—the roof of the world. The icy waters rush down from the towering peaks, through the rugged terrain of Afghanistan's Hindu Kush, and divide the arid wastes of the Kara Kum and Kyzyl Kum deserts. The now steamy waters end in a lackluster delta at the Aral Sea some fifteen-hundred miles from the snows of the Pamirs.

As it flows across Turkmenistan's northeastern bounder, the river meanders through six-hundred miles of shallow channels and sandbars. There are no raging white water rapids or dramatic water falls; only sluggish brown waters, as if the river's energy had been expended cascading down the Pamirs. It spans about a mile at its greatest width.

The Amudarya is landlocked in the vastness of the Asian continent, running nowhere. Its behavior is more temperamental than other rivers that eventually flow to the oceans. Historians have suggested that in antiquity one branch of it called the Uzboi flowed into the Caspian Sea. Like Turkmenistan's other landlocked river, the Murgap, the Amudarya slowly changed course over the centuries. The river held such life-sustaining power in the desert climate that whole cities were moved to follow its change in course.

When a geographic feature endures long enough, it under-goes several name changes depending on the people living near it. So it was for the Amudarya. At various times it was known as the Jaihun, Amul, Balk, Tuniderya, and the Oxus. It was a part of Greek, Persian, and Arab history and its ori-gins blur into myth. In his travels to Afghanistan, the Brit-ish historian Arnold Toynbee waxed poetic about the river and longed to catch a glimpse of it. Some biblical scholars theorized that it was the second river created in the Book of Genesis, the Gihad that flowed into Paradise.

To the Greeks, the river was known as the Oxus. Alexander the Great discovered it for the Western world in pursuit of his Persian foe, Besseus. Besseus fled Persia, crossed the Oxus for protection, and burned his boats on the north bank.

Alexander pursued, ordering his engineers to turn their animal hide tents into rafts. The crossing took five days. Bes-seus was captured, tried and sentenced by one of Alexander's generals to have both his nose and his ears cut off. While his armies were on the far side of the Oxus, Alexander con-quered the Sogdinian city of Maracanda (later known as Samarkand). He ended his march into western Asia on the southern bank of the Jaxartes (now the Syrdaria) at a settle-ment called, "Alexandria-the-Farthest." Beyond was the great expanse of the Asian Steppe that held the barbaric Scyth-ians. To Alexander's mind the Greeks had reached the edge of the civilized world.

In the early 8th Century, when Arab armies ventured across the river, they knew it as Jaihun, or "rushing river," a name still familiar to some older Turkmen today. When the Mongols pushed through, they swam their horses across. Ibn Battuta, who crossed its waters in the 14th Century, con-tinued to associate the Jaihun as one of the four rivers which flowed from Paradise. Some five centuries later, Peter the Great believed the Oxus was the source of large gold deposits and considered how he might colonize the land to extract its wealth.

Since Alexander, few Europeans had seen the Oxus, but it gained significance as a boundary in what became known as the "The Great Game"—the rivalry between Russia and England over control of Central Asia. Tsar Paul I ordered his Cossacks to march from Russia to India but admitted that his maps only went as far as the River Oxus. The march was ill fated, and before the Cossacks could reach the river, they were turned around with the news of Paul's assassination. The Russians vied for control for everything north of the Oxus, while the British occupied the territory from Afghanistan south to India. In 1825, a British veterinary surgeon, William Moorcroft, traveled far north of India in search of horses for the East India Company's cavalry. Near the modern-day boundaries of Afghanistan, Uzbekistan, and Turkmenistan, Moorcroft became the first Englishman to see the river. He crossed the Oxus, hoping to arrive in Bukhara and return with a fresh stock of horses. He returned empty-handed, only to die of fever and be buried near Balkh in Afghanistan within a day's ride to the river. The Russians and the English continued to make secret raids across the Amudarya, mapping territory and probing each other's strengths.

In the early 20th Century, the Russians adopted and re-popularized the ancient Farsi name for the river, calling it the Amudarya. The translation is unclear, but some think it a variant of "mother."

During the Cold War, the river served as an important boundary between the former Soviet Union and Afghanistan. In 1979, the Soviets invaded Afghanistan, driving military convoys of tanks and armored personnel carriers over the Amudarya's "Friendship Bridge" at Termez. When I walked the main bazaar of Ashgabat that summer, "war rugs" depicting the Soviet tanks were still for sale.

* * *

My drought tour began at the Ashgabat airport as I waited for the Turkmen Air flight to Dashoguz. As our flight was called and the passengers walked out to the Yak-40, I was approached by a very friendly Turkmen man who spoke excellent English. He took great interest in where I sat and where I stowed my bag. He even asked why I was going to Dashoguz.

President Niyazov had established a special commission in the Ministry of Foreign Affairs to monitor the activities of foreigners. I suspected this overly friendly traveler was KNB sent to "watch" the movements of the foreigner. I tried to deliver answers as vaguely as possible without being rude, and returned to reading my book, *Mission to Tashkent* (FM Bailley). It was about a British spy in Central Asia who was trying to evade the Checka, the Bolshevik secret police, shortly after the Communist revolution. This was not a happy coincidence. I hoped it would not send my minder the wrong message.

* * *

As we made our approach to Dashoguz, I could see the network of irrigation canals that fed the thirsty cotton fields. During Soviet times, Turkmenistan had been developed to keep the USSR self-sufficient in cotton production. Four of its five provinces were considered to be "cotton" provinces and, with irrigation from the Amudarya, it became one of the largest cotton producing regions in the world. Cotton is a water-hungry crop, and so it was a special challenge for a desert climate.

In keeping with the Soviet fascination for all things gigantic, they planned the Kara Kum Canal that would span two-thirds of the country and, when complete, would be the longest canal in the world. Built between 1959 and 1976, the canal was 900 miles long, with a pipeline extension that allowed the residents of the Caspian Sea town of Turkmen-bashi to brush their teeth with water from the Amudarya. The Kara Kum Canal and its offshoots were intended to irrigate over a million acres. After independence in 1991, Turkmenistan made plans to extend the canal and its network to irrigate over two and a half million acres. The canal and its reservoirs were almost like the creation of a second river since they held more water than the Amudarya. Most ambitious of all was a plan, announced by the President with great fanfare, to build a "Golden Lake" in the middle of the Kara Kum Desert.

Once on the ground, my friendly Turkmen shadow faded away somewhere in the Dashoguz terminal. I did not know how much he knew of my itinerary, but I expected I might see him or one of his colleagues before too long.

Pavel, our driver, met me with the office vehicle; a Chevy Suburban 2500 that he had driven up the day before. Pavel was half Russian and half Kazak but looked all Russian with wintry blue eyes. In the 1980's he performed his mandatory military service in Czechoslovakia during the years when the Soviet Red Army still existed. He was in his early forties and had a wife and nineteen-year-old daughter who he hoped could go to college in England.

An American contractor, Peter, who had grown up on a Wisconsin farm, and now managed our agricultural aid projects in Turkmenistan, joined me. Peter had close-cropped blond hair with a wiry build and seemed to be able to take naps even during the middle of a meeting. He had worked all over the world since leaving the Peace Corps in Nepal in the early 1970's. A mild-mannered gentleman approaching fifty, he was one of the few human beings in the world who has worked in both North Korea and Turkmenistan.

Rustam, a young Turkmen in his early twenties, a farmer with a shock of dark mahogany hair and piercing brown eyes, completed the group. He was an employee of Peter's organization, and he doubled as our Turkmen translator.

We started our excursion directly from the airport on a broken asphalt road that paralleled the Amudarya but seldom came within sight of it. Peter focused our attention on the low and irregular rows of green cotton plants. Sometimes small groups of women were bent over the rows weeding around the plants in the hot sun.

About twenty miles southeast of Dashoguz, the cotton fields become scattered and finally give way to desert. We drove parallel to a large canal. Its banks were so eroded, we initially confused it with a river. Surrounding us were mixed clumps of low, flat thorn bushes broken by stretches of sand dunes. Created by western winds, some were crescent shaped, called "barkhans." Many were larger than a two-story house.

"About a million acres of new desert appear every year in Central Asia," Peter said, looking at the dunes. "Its growth is second only to that of the Sahara and the Sehel. Plus, the Ministry of Agriculture has added to the problem by irrigating through a system of unlined canals."

We could see pools of water running along either side of the road.

"Nearly half the water leaches into the soil and forms salt marshes," Peter added. "The leakage increases salinization. The Turkmen inherited their canals from the Soviets, but they've continued to expand and dig more canals."

Beyond the pools of evaporating water were dry and cracked clay flats. They looked like sand-colored pools of ice that had cracked and refrozen. Turkmenistan was in a war with nature. It was trying to expand its irrigated lands into the desert. The Turkmen could win small battles, but nature specialized at playing the long game and winning. The sand dunes behaved as snowdrifts shaped by the wind.

Some had drifted over the road. Larry had warned me that he had tried to make this drive once before, but that Pavel had lost his nerve. This was Pavel's first test of adversity, so I watched his reactions closely.

Our route followed the Amudarya into Uzbekistan. We stopped at a lonely border checkpoint in Turkmenistan to have our exit recorded. The post was nothing more than a detached housing from an old military truck. Half a mile away, we stopped at the Uzbek checkpoint where young soldiers recorded the number on the Suburban's license plate. Ignoring the natural boundary of the Amudarya, the border zigzagged across both sides of the river, sometimes bringing both banks within the territory of Turkmenistan, other times within that of Uzbekistan.

* * *

High noon and the Suburban was stuck. Sand so heavily drifted across the road that a Soviet-made truck resembling a troop transport for the former Red Army was also stuck. The truck, coming from the opposite direction, tried to skirt the dune and drove off the shoulder of the road. The crew must have quickly realized their mistake when their rig lost all traction and sank down in the soft sand. The truck blocked the right shoulder of the road, forcing Pavel to try to bully his way through the drift in the road. The Suburban bogged down, came to a halt, and then backslid to within three or four inches of the big truck. Two heads bobbed up from the cab of the Soviet truck to see what the noise was. They had been sleeping, as if realizing that their situation was hopeless, but confident that help would come eventually.

Pavel's immediate reaction was to engage the dazed crew in a strident exchange in Russian. He sounded like a man mortally offended, as if our problem was their fault.

"Sir," Pavel said, "their driver has gone to get help, and the crew is not allowed to drive the truck."

Pavel decided he could free the Suburban by shoveling sand from around the wheels and shoving boards under the tires to gain traction. The setting had all the elements of a disaster movie: men stuck in a harsh desert—sun beating down—situation hopeless. Pavel's digging did nothing to help the Suburban, and no doubt we would soon be forced to ration radiator fluid for drinking water.

At our backs, I heard the deafening idle of a turbo-diesel engine. I turned around to view a KAMAZ—the largest truck I had seen on any road. Its huge knobby tires came up to my chest. Once the pride of the Soviet truck building industry, the KAMAZ sat as if it were a menacing, armor-plated dinosaur huffing diesel fumes. The driver eyed us distantly from high up in his tinted cab. Minutes later, a Toyota minivan with the lower grillwork torn off pulled up facing the KAMAZ from across the sand dune. The Toyota carried a load of Uzbek men with bone-colored skullcaps and women with colorful headscarves. Behind the Toyota, a gray Soviet-made four-wheel-drive pulled up. We now had a traffic jam in the middle of nowhere.

Meanwhile, Pavel attached two tow ropes to the back side of the Suburban and hooked them to the giant KAMAZ truck. Peter, Rustam, and I stood back a respectful distance—roughly judged to be outside of the ropes' whiplash range—and watched. The KAMAZ fished the three-quarter ton Suburban, the largest passenger vehicle produced in the U.S., out of the sand like a toy from a sandbox. The driver could not be bothered with a "thank you" for what to him amounted to a paltry effort. We had passed this lumbering behemoth some miles back with the smugness of upstarts in our shiny new American rig. Now its driver must be thinking about a Turkmen version of Aesop's fable of the tortoise and the hare. He had done us a big favor, and we were free, but still blocked by the drifts of sand.

A third van with small red-cross markings on the side, perhaps a military medical vehicle, pulled up on the opposite side of the drift. Young men piled out wearing remnants of uniforms. They looked like four men had been issued three uniforms and fought over their ensembles. One man wore sand-colored military pants and a white tank-top. Others were in civilian clothes and it was unclear whether they were soldiers or paramedics, but they had returned the driver of the marooned truck. We thought for a moment that now that the authorities had arrived to take charge, there would be progress. We were soon disappointed. There was only a general milling about, first around the sand drift, then around the embedded truck. Judging from the posturing and general demeanor of the men, I imagined their conversation was similar to what you might find among men in any American backwater:

In the first scene, the group looked at the sand drift.

First guy, "Yup, that's a big pile of sand."

Second guy, "Yup."

Others, "Yup."

In the second scene, the group turned to look at the truck.

First guy "Yup, that's a truck."

Second guy, "Yup."

Others, "Yup."

First guy, "That truck is stuck."

Second guy, "Yup."

Others, "Yup."

First guy, "Maybe we should do something?"

Second guy, with others, "I don't know? You think so?"

The driver of the trapped truck returned to its cab. The only help the soldiers offered was to watch. The driver turned the key but the starter failed to turn over the engine.

Impatiently, the driver of the gray four-wheel-drive van

revved up his engine and tried to force his way through the drift. No success. The van was returned onto pavement with the assistance of half a dozen pushing men. Then, it backed up like a high jumper trying to give himself a flying start, sped forward, veered off the road, climbed up the slope of the dune, over the top, past all the idled vehicles and back down to the road.

Everyone cheered.

Next, the white grill-less Toyota emptied its passengers. The long stream of Uzbek men and women looked like a small circus car that empties an improbable number of clowns. The Toyota climbed up and over the dunes also with great speed. The key was to keep moving over the hard pack of dunes, on the windward side of the road and avoiding the soft pack on the leeward side.

Pavel decided his manliness had been challenged, and we executed the same maneuver with only me as passenger. The Suburban climbed up the dune and back down and, after a moment's exhilaration, we realized we had come off the dune right in front of the stuck truck. Laughter erupted from the crowds on both sides. Pavel backtracked over the dune and repeated the maneuver. This time we cleared all obstacles and bolstered Pavel's confidence. Our party ran through the drift to reach the Suburban, and we drove on never knowing what became of the stranded truck.

After another 3 miles, we passed a semi-truck hauling fifty-foot lengths of pipe for natural gas. It too was stuck in a drift. Other drivers had collected to help. We moved along.

At a Turkmen border checkpoint, a white Corgi-like dog with a white-and-brown face barked warnings at the Suburban. Against the outside mud-brown concrete guardhouse sat a metal bed frame with rusted springs. A lone guard, maybe eighteen or nineteen, approached us cautiously to check our documents.

We passed a large reservoir. Judging from the water line on the banks, it looked like it was at about one-third of its capacity.

"A man-made drought," Peter suggested to no one in particular.

Midway between Dashoguz and Turkmenibad was the Russian-settled town of Darganata, an enclave of green fields. We stopped at the town bazaar for lunch and were introduced to flat bread that the locals called "soup-bread." It tore off in long, stringy pieces. The five of us devoured a whole loaf in moments.

Southeast of town, we drove up on a plateau that looked down on cotton and wheat fields and out past the Amudarya. After hours of seeing desert, our eyes had to become accustomed to the green vegetation. We turned onto a dirt road, and Pavel pointed us in the direction of the river. We stopped the Suburban at the edge of a bluff about one-hundred feet above the river. In the early evening light the Amudarya showed itself as a gently meandering river, its waters the color of weak chocolate milk. We climbed down the bluff on a rickety series of steps, to a wooden platform set just above the steep muddy bank. This was where a USAID-funded hydrological station was to be installed.

In 1932, the intrepid Swiss adventurer Ella Maillart talked her way onto *The Pelican*, a Soviet flat-bottom steamer, at Charjew, and journeyed up the Amudarya on her way to Khiva. Near where we stood, the *Pelican* ran aground on one of the river's many shifting sandbars. During the night, the ship's crew was on watch for "basmatchi" or bandits that still roamed the area despite Soviet control. Ms. Maillart described these same bluffs from her vantage point on the steamer. She ate a meal of local pheasant with a Soviet hydrographer returning from mapping the Amudarya. Even then, the Soviets understood the importance of the river.

The current was barely perceptible and could only be seen by looking for small ripples and eddies near the banks. I knelt down and extended my arm, as if I were reaching out to shake hands. The water wet my dusty hand and swirled around it, making a small eddy.

* * *

We pressed on in our drive. In the darkness outside Turkmenibad, the Suburban was stopped at an internal checkpoint. This time, a uniformed officer with a man in plain clothes, wearing a square-cut leather jacket, the same type of jacket favored by my KNB minder on the airplane, approached us. Peering through the driver's side window, the two authorities repeatedly asked Pavel where we had come from. When he said Dashoguz, they repeated the question several more times as if they did not believe us. They asked for our passports. I always found this interesting since we were traveling inside Turkmenistan and a passport was normally a document needed for international travel. The plainclothes official asked if another member of our Embassy was in the vehicle. He was not. The officials told Pavel they wanted to inspect the Suburban.

"You want a scandal," I heard Pavel say in Russian.

The officials continued to peer into the window with flashlights.

"If you have finished with our passports, please return them," I told Pavel to translate.

The official understood before translation. Evidently not willing to risk a "scandal," the men returned our passports and we traveled to Turkmenibad.

"Maybe they were just testing us?" Pavel said to the group.

One thing that had not changed since Ella Mailart's time was what she called the "poisonous bureaucrats," who caused her numerous delays by questions, permissions, and restrictions, all to travel inside one country. Once the Turkmen led a nomadic existence on the Steppes of Central Asia; now they needed permission to travel from their home province.

* * *

We spent the night in Turkmenibad at a makeshift guesthouse. It was a room for rent in a Soviet block apartment building. Our hostess, a pleasant matronly woman, said most of the locals still referred to Turkmenibad by its old name, Charjew, meaning the point where four roads meet. Silk Road caravans had traveled this route, as had later Turkmen raiding parties, carrying their Persian captives to Bukhara for sale in the slave markets.

Charjew was an important crossing point for the river. It was somewhere near here that Alexander's army launched its amphibious tents to reach the north bank in pursuit of Besseus. The town itself was charmless, without trees. Most of its buildings were still the Soviet cement block style. Even the Amudarya did little to nothing to change the town's stark appearance.

In 1888, English Lord Curzon crossed the Amudarya at Turkmenibad on the Russian-run Trans-Caspian railway. From his train compartment he was given to a rapturous description, writing, "there in the moonlight gleamed before us the broad bosom of the mighty river from the glaciers of the Pamir rolls its 1,500 miles of current down to the Aral Sea." He went on to invoke a poem by Mathew Arnold, *Sohrab and Rustum*, which tells the story of a legendary Persian warrior who by tragic mistake slays his own son on the banks of the Oxus.

Sixty-three years earlier, Curzon's countryman, Moorcroft, the veterinarian, had crossed downriver from here by ferry. He was less poetic, saying matter-of-factly that "the banks were low, and the soil loose, like those of the Ganges, and the water was similarly discolored by sand."

My own observation was closer to Moorcroft's.

* * *

In the morning we drove to the eastside of Turkmenibad, to its principal bazaar. Looming up on a small ridge behind was a decaying ancient fortress of mud walls.

"It is bad luck to go inside," Rustam said.

"Do you know anything about it?" I asked.

"It once belonged to the Emir of Bukhara, in Uzbekistan," Rustam said. In what appeared a common pattern among young Turkmen, Rustam, who had grown up in Turkmenibad, could offer no other history.

Peter guided us to the field of a local wheat farmer he had worked with on one of his irrigation projects. The farmer walked us into the field and showed us his crop with its stunted stalks. Peter pulled one of the heads off a stalk and crumbled the grains in his hand. Even to my untrained eye, the grains looked anemic.

"We were to have five irrigations of the field last month but we only had one," the farmer explained in Turkmen through Rustam.

As we talked, a white Volga sedan with shaded windows pulled up the dirt road beside the field and sat about fifty yards away. The moment we left the field, a man in a black leather jacket stepped out of the Volga and approached the farmer.

"No doubt KNB," Peter said. "They probably want to question him about what we talked about. It seems information about the wheat crop has become sensitive even though the Government is reporting record-setting harvests."

"What do you think the penalties will be for his conversation?" I asked Peter.

"I don't know, but we've become poison for the local farmers," replied Peter. "It seems clear that our presence is hurting them more than helping them."

Two seasons later, the President had announced a record grain harvest of 2.5 million tons. The actual figure reported by local experts was 480 thousand tons—one-fifth of what was claimed. Meanwhile, we heard reports that police units went from farm to farm forcibly seizing any grain they might find, reminiscent of Soviet collectivization of the 1920's.

Peter and I decided the second half of the river drive must wait. What we had seen in the canals and reservoirs and fields, and heard from the farmers, had convinced us there was a shortage of water. This was not a drought for lack of rain; it seemed more that Turkmenistan's ambitious irrigation system was breaking down. Nature was reclaiming the desert it had created.

I asked Pavel if he could make the drive back to Ashgabat before dark.

"Koneshna," (of course) he replied.

* * *

The drive from Turkmenibad to Mary was monotonous miles of desolate desert scrub. From the comfort of the air-conditioned Suburban I looked out into the harshness of the desert and tried to imagine how many scorpions might live between the edge of the road and the horizon.

During the Great Game, a British Army Lieutenant, Richmond Shakespear, had traveled this same stretch of desert from Merv to the Oxus. He led a military reconnaissance expedition from Herat to Khiva, and declared this stretch of desert the most perilous of his mission. Where we in the Suburban cruised down the ribbon of crumbling black-top confident that we would reach Ashgabat that evening, Shakespear reported there was no perceptible trail. The only markings were the bones of animals and the occasional skull of a camel that some helpful traveler had stuck on a thorn bush along the way. Had it not been for an intelligent local guide who claimed to see the trail, even at night, Shakespear declared the whole party would have been lost and died of thirst in the severe heat.

Between Mary and Ashgabat, I asked Pavel to stop in the barren landscape next to a giant sign reading "Kaka" marking the etrap by that name. I am sure there are many more rigorous philosophical methods used to define "absurdity" but at that moment, a giant sign announcing "Kaka" at the edge of a flat, desolate landscape was at least a good illustration. My piece of the absurdity was to have my picture taken next to the sign.

* * *

Bad things always seemed to happen during my absence from Ashgabat. I returned to the news that the guards on compound had captured a cobra in the backyard of our pre-fabricated townhouse. The snake turned out to be a baby and was put into an empty soda bottle. For the guards it was an amusement, but that evening there was much excitement in our household. Eileen suggested we reconsider whether we should live in a place where poisonous snakes sunned themselves on the same patch of grass where our two-year-old played.

Charlotte was unscathed and oblivious to the weighty discussion. Instead, she had brought together the two diverse worlds of 20th Century Big Band music and Uzbek folklife in our living room. As Eileen and I talked about the hazards of deadly snakes, Charlotte danced in a circle to Glenn Miller's *Pennsylvania 6-5000* on the CD player while wildly "playing" a six-stringed Uzbek rebop we had bought her on a trip to Bukhara.

* * *

The next month, I returned to Turkmenibad to complete the second half of the Amudarya drive. This time accompanied by Mike, an American hydrologist, and Tanya, a Kazak-Russian civil engineer, both of whom worked with USAID's water projects. Mike and Tanya had been working to install hydrological stations in Central Asia to accurately measure the water flow of the Amudarya. Our goal was to talk with local officials and visit the head works of the Kara Kum Canal.

The trip began in a Soviet-made Tu-154, which was the usual sauna and smell-o-rama of odors. The planes did not run air conditioning, so in the hot July sun, 150 passengers baked inside the metal fuselage.

* * *

In Turkmenibad, Mike and I met with a local water official who gave us a list of reasons why we could not visit the canal head works. The reasons were many and varied and included the fact that it was too close to the Afghan border, and the "Taliban might decide to shoot at you Americans."

That evening we attended a business dinner at a canal pumping station that supplied water to Bukhara and the surrounding area. Our hosts were an Uzbek and a Turkmen who had joint authority over the distribution of the water. The Amudarya was the life of Turkmenistan and Uzbekistan. The meat, vegetables, fruit, and *plov* served in ridiculous quantities were the result. Our hosts initiated generous rounds of toasts. After the obvious toasts to friendship they became carried away, devising the flimsiest reasons to drink. They challenged me to make as many toasts as possible.

I tried to spill every other vodka toast under the table but my hosts watched me closely. I lost track of time and only remembered returning to the makeshift guesthouse. I fell into a blurry, unsatisfying sleep, the type resulting from the combination of alcohol, fatigue, and heat exhaustion.

* * *

In the morning, we hired a local driver, Murad, who met us at the guesthouse. He was a retired Aeroflot pilot in his fifties. He had a row of gold front teeth highlighted by a dark

Turkmen complexion, made darker by years spent under the sun of the Kara Kum desert. Within minutes, I was in the front passenger seat and Mike and Tanya in the back while our driver steered his Lada westward, effortlessly speeding over some of the worst roads in the country. He drove with gusto, skillfully staying between the margins of negligence and recklessness. I reached for the seat belt but he urged me not to use it with a wave of his hand.

"Ne rebotet!" (it doesn't work) he exclaimed. The explanation did not come with the tone of an apology but with the attitude of, "Isn't it great, you don't need to bother with these pesky things." I had to pretend we were not really passing eighteen-wheeler trucks on blind corners at 80 mph or swerving to avoid lumbering Soviet-era dump trucks, which approached us head-on. I tried to imagine that I was at the Smithsonian's Air and Space Museum IMAX Movie Theater watching "Turkmenistan Highway Adventure!"

With casual regard for other traffic, we attempted rudimentary discussion of his days as an airplane pilot.

"Chuck Yeager," I said hoping this modern hero of aviation might break the language barrier and trigger a look of recognition.

Murad gave me a confused look.

"He broke the sound barrier," I said and added a "BOOM!" with a hand motion.

"Nyet," said Murad. A pilot from Soviet Georgia had broken the sound barrier. Soviets held all the important firsts in aviation.

"At least," he allowed, "this was what I learned during the days of the Soviet Union."

In an effort at diplomacy, I steered the conversation to what I knew was a great Soviet first.

"Yuri Gagarian," I said.

Murad nodded enthusiastically.

As we talked aviation and cosmonauts, our route took us along the south bank of the Amudarya River, past a series of crumbling 14th Century fortresses on either side of the road. Most were constructed of thick mud walls on a rise of land. Some were no more than mounds of dried mud, their secrets sinking deeper into obscurity. Only one had a monument marking its place in history.

Murad pointed to the mud and rock fortress and explained that Saya, a Turkmen poet, once lived inside its sullen walls. In this part of the world, poets had once held higher status than sheiks. Poets like Saya, Makhtumkuli and others had carried the soul of the Turkmen through their oral traditions. The 18th Century poet Makhtumkuli is perhaps more revered than any other figure in Turkmen history.

Before leaving on this trip, Jamala from our office staff gave me what may have been Makhtumkuli's most famous poem. Jamala was in her late forties and the mother of two grown boys but was filled with the inquisitive energy of a wide-eyed college freshman. She had grown up in an academic household where her father had been a professor at Turkmenistan's top university during Soviet times. She wanted me to have the poem as "inspiration" for my trip:

The Pains of Love

Love caught fire within my heart, and burned and blazed.
Smoke whirling in the wind whipped me like something crazed.
Fate caught me, spinning me upon its wheel.
Who came to see me through the eyes of real desire?
Separation was a storm - both flood and fire.

Swept on, I gained the shores of love, shipwrecked - so null
Real and unreal were hurricanes within my skull.
I felt exhausted, lost in wonderment.
When love unsheathed its dagger yes, I caught its blade!
Love stripped me naked, left stranded without shade.

My body held no strength, my corpse no uttering soul
I staggered round, confused and far from whole,
Not weary or alert, alive or dead.
A cloud of sorrow sank to hide my sacrifice,
As destiny's key turned and locked me in its vice.

I had to fight to make grief's specter disappear;
But Love instructed me and made the problem clear
Love sorrowed and assisted me to heal.
When beauty bloomed, it brought spring joys of a fresh start.
I have to say all this, dear friends! It broke my heart.

Oh, hopeful slave to the beloved's charms, whereby
I lost my heart! A songbird of sweet tongues was I -
Encaged! But separation scorched my soul.
Then yearning burned me up, to ash was turned my mind.
And Makhtumkuli life was tossed upon the wind.

The power and strength of the poem seemed in stark contrast to the bleakness of the surroundings. Like the colorful carpets made in the desolation of the desert, the creative powers of Makhtumkuli seem to be a counterweight to his surroundings.

Clustered around the fortresses were cemeteries with white plaster above-ground crypts. Like so many other Turkmen I was to encounter, Murad knew Soviet history but there was little else he could tell me about the meaning of these fortresses and Turkmenistan's own past.

By mid-morning, we passed a small no-name oasis with lots of trees. The proprietors of the covered *shashliek* stands were still collecting scraps of gnarled wood to begin the day's cooking. Charpoys, raised wooden platforms, sat in the cool spaces waiting for their customers to take tea and *plov*. A few trucks had already parked along the side of the road, their crews sipping tea or catching some sleep.

Some twenty-five miles before Kerki, later renamed "Attamurat" to honor the birthplace of the President's father, we stopped at the temple of Astana Baba, considered one of the holiest sites in Turkmenistan. Surrounded by a low brick wall, the shrine was made up of three clustered domes. Inside its brick archway, three generations of one family sat in the shade of a mulberry tree. An old man with a white Ahab-like beard and a small embroidered hat sat quietly presiding over the group. He and his wife dressed in contrast to his eight-year-old grandson, who dressed like an inner-city boy, complete with a baseball cap with a logo endorsing an American brand of gym shoes. The family served as unofficial caretakers. The boy, who acted as a guide, unlocked the wooden doors to the shrine, said to be from the 12th Century. Our young guide spoke only Turkmen, and the Russian-speaking members of our group could barely understand enough Turkmen to bridge the gap. Of what we saw, we could only guess at the history. We were shown a series of three chambers, each with a brick tomb covered with a white sheet. The three dead were all of the same family. In the last chamber, women had left strands of ribbons and replicas of small baby cradles as fertility offerings. At the end of our muted tour, our party made donations of Manat to the boy, who said a short, hurried blessing as he took each one.

Outside Kerki we stopped at a police checkpoint. The scene presented a picture of relaxed activity. Two officers, one a policeman, the other a border guard, sat at a rough wooden table in the shade of a tree. An old man with a white beard peddled his bicycle around the lowered red and white pole barrier. No one paid him any attention. The scene had almost a festive look. It was as if they were preparing to sell raffle tickets at a neighborhood block party later on a summer afternoon. Two Afghani men in *shalwar kamis*, long flowing shirts that looked like oversized old-fashioned nightshirts, approached the checkpoint on foot. A van pulled up with about ten people inside, and the border guard casually approached to ask for their documents. After twenty minutes of examining our passports and permits, they raised the barrier and we drove through.

Kerki itself looked jolly relative to other Turkmen towns that often seemed like nothing more than blocks of concrete bunkers. The streets were smaller and windier. A three-story building of intricate brickwork fortified almost an entire block. It was built during Tsarist times and had been the center of Kerki's small, but prosperous, Jewish colony. Small Jewish colonies had survived here, in Bukhara and elsewhere in Central Asia since the Middle Ages. Many had migrated to Israel and now, there were only two or three families left.

South of Kerki, the ruins of another old fortress sat atop a hill and looked down on the city's small airport. We paralleled the Kara Kum Canal, which was no longer surrounded by green fields but instead surrounded by harsh desert. For such a desolate stretch of road there was a large volume of semi-trucks – Volvos, Mercedes, even a U.S.-made Mack truck, all with Arabic license plates headed in the direction of the Afghan border.

We stopped at Lake Zeit, a reservoir lake created by a Soviet-era sluice, part of the canal system. The sluice looked like a small dam, and it had created a lake of wetlands, its level regulated by the massive hydraulic doors of the sluice. We climbed the steps to the top of sluice and stood over its metal grates. The water below agitated with tremendous energy, as if we were looking through a cage at a raging, wild animal angry over the attempt to confine and control it. At the opening of the sluice, a group of boys fished with homemade fishing poles. They had caught large, prehistoric-looking fish, some over three feet long. The fish looked like a cross between a catfish and an eel. They kept the fish flopping around in shallow mud puddles. Each boy pulled his catch out to display the mud-colored creatures to us. It quickly became a competition as each boy mugged for our camera, vying with the others to show us who had the most prized fish. Lake Zeit was a cool island of blue in the midst of desert.

We backtracked to a rickety pontoon bridge that crossed the canal. Our car of five passengers scraped its oil pan on the bridge with the weight of our load. Someone had tried to cushion the blows to the cars' undersides with piles of straw and mulberry leaves. Next to the bridge were half a dozen rusting hulks of ships and two barge-mounted dredges. Mike and I dubbed this the "Kara Kum Navy."

We arrived at the head works of the Kara Kum Canal by early afternoon. For Mike, a hydrologist, this was a milestone. This was the entry point for the world's longest canal, like one of the seven wonders of world for water engineers. Now he was able to see what his colleagues had only studied in books.

We walked to the edge of the canal to hear the roar of the water as it entered the canal with the same agitation as at Lake Zeit. The mad waters created a balmy mist of cool air that gave momentary relief from the desert temperature of 115°F. Mike began taking pictures of the massive sluices that fed water into the canal at the rate of over 130,000 gallons a second.

Cameras could easily create a lot of excitement in Turkmenistan, particularly near large civil engineering sites like the Kara Kum. I could see a man and woman excitedly waving at us as they ran from the caretaker's house. They were clearly nervous that foreigners had unexpectedly driven into the grounds and were taking pictures. They wanted us to stop. We were asked to come and have tea and homemade preserves under the shade of mulberry trees in the caretaker's back yard. Here we relaxed in a small spot of serenity in the extreme northeastern corner of the country. We were only a mile or two from Afghanistan. While the caretaker disappeared, I assumed to call the authorities, his wife continued to offer us tea and raisins. Half an hour later a man wearing a well-groomed *tilpek* drove up the entrance to the canal headworks in a shiny royal blue motorcycle with sidecar.

* * *

The official escorted us back to Kerki. It seemed they wanted simply to get us out of the area before they had to explain to others that uninvited foreigners had showed up to take pictures. As a parting request, however, the official allowed Mike and me to have our pictures taken in his motorcycle with sidecar.

* * *

In Turkmenibad, I met a pilot who was a relative of a Turkmen colleague. He brought me to his home. In keeping with Turkmen standards of generous hospitality, his whole family greeted me. His wife offered me slices of watermelon and a yogurt drink. I tried a sweet red Turkmen wine that tasted like Port. A woman and son who were neighbors arrived. The son had just come back from his senior year in high school in Connecticut. I was a total stranger to them moments ago but was immediately warmed by their quick friendship. The father gave me two Soviet coins, one with Lenin and the other with Popov, "inventor of the radio." He then walked me to the airport, and I boarded the evening plane for Ashgabat.

We took off in the twilight, and out of the snug cabin of the Yak-40 I could see the gray-green ribbon of the Amudarya, visible in the evening haze. It was once the stuff of intrigue and myth to Europeans who had been denied even a glimpse of it. Now I had observed it up close and touched its lazy waters. I studied the river one more time, tracing its path until it disappeared into the purple shadows of the horizon.

JOURNEY 8

On the Trail of Saints and Russians

Krasnovodsk is one of the hottest, most deserted places in the world.
The mountains are dead; there is no water in them.
Rain scarcely ever falls, and the earth is only sand and salt.
--Stephen Graham, Through Central Asia, 1914

Five is a recurring number in Turkmenistan. There are five *welayatlar*, the Turkmen flag shows five *guls* (medallion-like designs), representing the five major tribes and displays five stars over a crescent moon. The national seal contains the five tribal *guls*. Then there is another state symbol—a five-headed, golden eagle. None of the Turkmen friends I asked could tell me what particular significance the number five held.

* * *

On the morning of Nowruz Bairam (Farsi for "New Year's Day"), I traveled to Balkan, the fifth and final province of my Turkmen journeys. As Turkmenistan's western-province, it borders the Caspian Sea and had traditionally been the stronghold of the second most powerful Turkmen tribe, the Yomut.

Guljahan, who worked for a USAID partner organization as a librarian, a rare profession in Turkmenistan since there were almost no libraries in the country, knew of my interest in local history. She was a Turkmen woman in her early twenties who always spoke English with a smile on her face. Guljahan traced her family and tribal roots to a Yomut village in Balkan. A week before the holiday, Guljahan volunteered to show Dovelet and me to the holy shrine of a Turkmen saint, Paraw Bibi. It was the one of three visits that brought me to Balkan.

Driving west out of Ashgabat, the morning presented a blue sky with the sun shining through two cloudbanks, creating a "miracle" effect with its rays. A fresh breeze whipped along a flotilla of small clouds. The Government had declared a national holiday for Nowruz Bairam. It arrived every year at the beginning of spring on the vernal equinox and was the beginning of the year for the people in parts of Central Asia, particularly Iranians and Kurds. The holiday had become much more celebrated in recent years since Turkmen independence. Tradition said that Nowruz went as far back in human history as thousands of years ago to when Indo-Iranians moved from hunting to domestication of livestock and a more settled lifestyle. The weather and the holiday seemed to offer a positive blessing to our trip.

As I drove, Guljahan explained that Paraw Bibi was a beautiful woman devoted to Islam. When her village was attacked by pagan invaders the leader of the attackers wanted to marry Paraw Bibi. She tried to save herself and escape in the mountains above her village. She had no hope of escape, but then the mountain opened up and swallowed Paraw Bibi inside. A shrine now sits on the site where she disappeared into the mountain.

"How long ago was this?" I asked.

"No one knows," said Guljahan.

Central Asian scholar David Tyson, one of the few Westerners to study shrine pilgrimage, described it as an example of the unusual brand of Sufi Islam that had endured in the rural areas of Turkmenistan. Tyson traced the origin of the local pilgrimages back to pre-Islamic times, blending local folklore with Islam. Believers from all over Turkmenistan made pilgrimages to Paraw Bibi, where they sought a blessing by offering prayers and leaving scraps of fabric on trees or on bricks of the structures to ask the saint to intercede in matters of fertility, disease, and other illnesses. I had visited other sites like Astana Baba and Khoja Yusup Baba at ancient Merv that also had cultic offerings but had not realized their significance to the Turkmen. Turkmen Islam is marked by the practice of pilgrimages to saints' shrines as well as to sacred trees, rocks, and streams, which are associated with saints, Muslim or otherwise. As at other Turkmen shrines, pilgrims at Paraw Bibi believed in the power of the saint to assist in fertility or cure insanity.

We turned south off the main road that led all the way to the Turkmenbashi City, the country's one port on the Caspian Sea, and drove through the village of Paraw Bibi. Guljahan directed me to a dirt parking area within the shadow of the Kopet Dag Mountains.

"There is Paraw Bibi's shrine," said Guljahan, pointing to a simple whitewashed mausoleum-like house halfway up a rocky mountainside. It was a small dot of smooth white set in the fold of a craggy brown mountain.

At the base of the mountain path was a one-story building that served as a sort of visitor's center. Guljahan covered her head with a scarf and took us inside to kneel before a young woman who pronounced a short blessing on our group. Outside the building was a watermelon-shaped stone.

"This is said to be the same stone from the time of Paraw Bibi," said Guljahan. "The pilgrims use it to "detect sin.""

The idea was that two people placed their thumbs under the stone; if the stone rotates those balancing it had committed no sin. Dovelet and I placed our thumbs under it. At first nothing happened, but then it began to feel a bit like playing with a Ouija board game. After a few minutes, our thumb pressure became uneven and the stone became unsteady and bobbed slightly. Guljahan claims she saw it spin. I suppose to say otherwise would have made her a bad hostess. She would not want to say, "The American has sin. We better throw him off the mountainside."

We climbed the path to the shrine to find other "miracle stones." Near the shrine were impressions said to be Paraw Bibi's hands and knees left in stone.

We watched as what appeared to be a mother and daughter took turns kneeling in the impressions and reaching to put their hands in the contours. It was like watching a brief game of Twister. At all Turkmen shrines it was important to touch sacred stones.

Standing before the impression, Dovelet told me to kneel.

"Maybe it will help you and Eileen have another child," he said showing his gold teeth.

"Yeah but isn't this for the woman?" I asked. "I don't see any men doing this. I think this would be messing with the power of the Paraw Bibi."

Guljahan pointed to another stone up the mountain path about the shape of a rugby ball.

"It is said to be a melon that Paraw Bibi had been about to eat," Guljahan said. "She was about to cut the melon when the enemies attacked and she threw it down to escape. The melon turned into stone."

A line formed at the door, mostly of women with children. Dusty shoes and sandals were piled in front of the entrance. The inner room was an octagonal shape and dimly lit only by natural light from the open doorway. Families knelt on the felt mats saying prayers. Women hoping for children filled the room and left miniature cradles. Then everyone went silent. Guljahan gestured to a natural passage in the mountain. It was actually a very narrow cave where Paraw Bibi is said to have entered into the mountain. Many of the young women queued up to climb inside, in near darkness, and recited prayers to the spirit of Paraw Bibi. The atmosphere was solemn, like being in a church.

I stepped outside into bright sunlight intensified by the whitewashed walls of the shrine. At the entrance to the shrine, a woman in her sixties asked if she and her family of six could be photographed with me, using my camera. Why would she want me to take a picture with my camera, a picture I had no way sending to her?

"She told her family that you will take an image of her family back to America," Guljahan said. Somehow this would bring the woman and her family good luck.

There was a mountain stream that amounted to a trickle of water, but Guljahan said, "It comes to life whenever there is a rainfall or the snow melts."

Hiking down the mountain trail, we were met by three young girls carrying bouquets of yellow wildflowers. They must have been about four, six, and eight. The oldest introduced herself as "Lela" and, seeing my camera, asked if she and her two sisters could be photographed with my two Turkmen friends. Their faces beamed with a light of unfettered happiness. They had been running up and down the mountain path as if they were three beautiful little sprites whose duty it was to welcome visitors to the shrine of Paraw Bibi. The girls handed Guljahan the wild flower bouquets and ran off laughing.

As the three ran down the path ahead of us, Guljahan heard them say in Turkmen, "If you are ever in Nebit Dag come visit us."

When we drove off, we could see them running through

a field of wildflowers that bloom for only a few days during the spring. They looked back at our car and gave us one final spirited wave.

* * *

On Halloween I returned to Balkan. This time I flew to Turkmenbashi City, Balkan's provincial seat, to attend a conference of local civic organizations that were receiving support from USAID. Until recently, Turkmenbashi City was known as Krasnovodsk, literally "red water." It was the oldest Russian-founded city in Turkmenistan and was known to the Turkmen as Shagadam, "first step of the king," because it was the first place where Peter the Great's representatives landed. Now, like other cities and towns, it had been renamed in honor of the President.

I was traveling with Svetlana, a colleague who worked for one of USAID's partners. Svetlana was an ethnic Russian woman with sad blue eyes, and a well-educated mother of grown children whose quiet persistence had helped USAID organize its activities in the face of government obstacles and harassment. She was responsible for organizing the workshop in Turkmenbashi City.

When we boarded the Yak-40, I saw a portrait of the President bolted to the front bulkhead of the cabin. Six olive drab duffel bags filled the overhead bin. They had all the right dimensions to contain parachutes. I settled into my seat and asked Svetlana if I could borrow her Russian-made pen to make entries in my journal. She shared the pen but then became slightly nervous when I started to write.

"Oh, Yak-40, this is a very good plane," Svetlana volunteered.

For a moment I wondered if the pen would automatically translate my English words into Russian. After an hour, we still had not taken off. I had been writing the whole time, but the pen still wrote in English. Without any announcement, we were herded off the plane back into the airport.

From inside the terminal, I watched for some clue as to the delay. The tarmac at Turkmenbashi Airport was normally quiet. I never saw more than one plane in motion at a time. There were no luggage carts or aircraft taxing to and from gates. The only activity was from a battered old yellow refueling truck that pulled up to a second plane. It resembled the truck in the movie *Duel* that chased Dennis Weaver through the American southwest before driving off a cliff—only this truck looked post-cliff. Its front fender was mangled, hanging down at a hazardous angle, and half of the engine compartment door was missing, exposing the grease-encrusted diesel. I hoped the Yak-40 was maintained with greater care.

After another hour, we reboarded the plane without explanation. The Yak-40 arced into the desert skies and headed west toward the Caspian Sea.

* * *

Since the time of Peter the Great, the Russians had looked for a way to gain a foothold in western Turkmenistan. The Yomut tribe, probably the second most important tribe in Turkmenistan, occupied the area as far north as Dashoguz and in the south near Kyzilarvat. To the east were their rivals, the powerful Tekkes. In 1714, a representative of Peter the Great met leaders of the Turkmen tribes who agreed to allow the Russians access to gold mining concessions in exchange for protection. Because of Peter's death soon after, the agreement was never implemented.

In the 19th Century, the Russians began to look for a better way to open up communications with the remote areas of Central Asia. The Russians attempted to establish a series of forts on the eastern shore of the Caspian. The forts were abandoned after a combination of harsh climate and tribal attacks. In 1869, the Russians sent a military ship on a clandestine mission to try again to build a fortress on the eastern side of Caspian. This was during the Great Game between Russia and England, and secrecy was important. To avoid detection by the British, the Russian Commander was under orders not to clash with the local Turkmen tribes. The Russians departed from the Petrovsk on the Caucasian side of the Caspian. They landed in a natural harbor on the barren shore some miles below where the last Russian fort had been abandoned in 1859 after being attacked by the Turkmen. On the north side of the harbor they began laying a stone foundation for a stronger and more substantial fort. This was the start of Krasnovodsk.

In 1874, the Yomut, the dominant Turkmen tribe of the Caspian region, agreed to assist the Russians with building a rail line in exchange for Russian protection. The Russian-Yomut relationship incited threats from the Tekkes to exterminate them. In an attempt to protect the Yomuts and to expand their foothold from the shore of the Caspian, the Russians battled the Tekkes in 1875 and 1877. The Tekkes fought ferociously, and the Russians were never able to move effectively beyond the Yomut settlement of Kyzilarvat. The Tekkes still controlled the central region all the way east to the Amudarya River and Afghanistan.

Not until 1881, after the Russian General Skobeloff crushed the Ahal Tekkes at the battle of Goeke Deppe (20 miles from present-day Ashgabat), did the Russians start the Trans-Caspian Railway. It was intended to link Central Asia with Russia and Siberia and solidify Russian control over Central Asia. Just as the arm of the Kara Kum Canal would later bring the waters of Amudarya west across Turkmen territory, the Trans-Caspian would bring passengers east to the Amudarya. The first leg of the rail line only got as far as Kyzilarvat, 145 miles from the Caspian, within the safety of the Russian's Yomut allies. When the Merv Tekkes finally submitted to Russian rule in 1884, the remaining rail line was completed. It ran to the Russian garrison town of Ashgabat, along the Persian border, east to Merv, and then veered northeast to Charjew where it crossed the Amudarya River into Uzbekistan. The railway totaled 650 miles through desert terrain.

Every railroad tie and spike had to be transported down the Caspian and across the desert. The barren, treeless wastes offered nothing for the construction. In some stretches, however, the terrain was so flat and featureless that construction crews could lay track at night. The biggest challenge was the shifting sand that covered the tracks in places. The railway was officially under military control until the collapse of the Soviet Union in 1991; but in 1896, it began offering daily trains from Krasnovodsk. During the height of the Great Game, one American observer wrote that the railway terminus of the Trans-Caspian made Krasnovodsk one of the most important towns in Central Asia.

Krasnovodsk was how most Europeans entered Turkmenistan, usually by way of a ferry from Baku on the western coast of the Caspian. Krasnovodsk was never a destination. It was usually a transfer point to the Trans-Caspian Railroad.

The Europeans and Americans who ventured to the town consistently gave it poor reviews.

In 1885, Henry Landsdell, a British adventure writer found it to be a "sorry place" and "never saw such a town for which nature had provided so scarcely. The population left to its own resources must speedily starve." Everything had to be brought in. He could not understand why the Russians had built a fort here. There were no fresh water wells. All water had to be distilled from the Caspian through a very labor intensive, inefficient means. At the time, he reported a population described as "400 Persians and Armenians, and 1,000 Russians (800 of whom were soldiers)."

A trickle of adventure writers and curiosity seekers that followed found nothing positive about Krasnovodsk—except for the train station:

The town itself is a mere collection of mean little one-story flat-roofed houses…the train station is the only architectural feature of the place.

--J.T. Woolrych Perowne on a Cook's Tour, 1898.

A Tombstone miner would feel at home here, resembles a mining town on the 'Nitrate Coast' of Chile. [The train station, however, was] a handsome building of Oriental design with alternate courses of dark and light gray stone.

--Eleroy Curtiss, The Heart of Central Asia, 1911

As a town, Krasnovodsk scarcely exists. Outside the station there is a square planted with dusty tamarisks, but the place appears to be used more as a public latrine than a public garden…behind the station a few small eating houses, very dirty and very full of flies, and a few squalid shops.

--Ethel Mannin, writer, 1935

The Soviets must have agreed. Krasnovodsk was bleak enough to serve as a place of exile. In 1942, Stalin banished the first President of independent Lithuania here.

The best review offered was in 1991, by Central Asian expert Kathleen Hopkirk, who found its people "the kindest and most helpful of any in the Soviet Union."

* * *

My first impression of Turkmenbashi City was not much better than my predecessors'—it was as if our plane had landed in the ninth circle of industrial hell. The drive from the airport took us through a wasteland littered with rusting hulks of machinery, cast-off refinery equipment, piles of concrete rubble, and unidentifiable debris baked by furnace-like temperatures. I looked at a corroded steel oil derrick on its side and wondered what catastrophe had caused workers to abandon it. As if to complete the geography of this hell-ish world, we passed a small lake that was a mixture of oil and other refinery pollutants held back from the waters of the Caspian by an earthen dike. The New Jersey Meadow-lands might have seemed like Yellowstone National Park by comparison.

The Balkan region was rich in fossil fuels. Turkmenistan sits atop one of the world's largest natural gas reserves as well as a modest deposit of oil. As early as the 1880's, 3,000 springs of "naphtha" were reported on the Island of Che-lekan. The first wells were started on the island in 1909 and development continued under the Soviets throughout west-ern Turkmenistan and offshore into the Caspian. Since its peak production in the 1970's, much of the oil equipment was neglected in favor of natural gas development. When equipment broke down or was no longer needed, the state-run oil industry cast it aside anyhow as if on the landscape was one giant trash can. Maybe the barren scenery rein-forced the Soviet idea that there was no environment worth protecting.

Our official guesthouse was a 12 mile drive outside the city limits of the Turkmenbashi City. The whitewashed four-story structure sat behind a low concrete wall above a rocky shore of the Caspian. The guesthouse and nearby *dachas* from Soviet days were the closest thing that Turkmenistan had to a resort. A sea breeze blew a slightly salty smell. The sea had a prehistoric feel to it that terrified me. The Turk-men talked about swimming in the Caspian, but I had no urge even to dip a toe into its mysterious waters. I thought of slimy, dark eels and giant, monstrous sturgeon that might lurk beneath its choppy waters.

Geologists consider the Caspian an unusual body of water. It has been called a survivor of former oceans and is believed by some to have once flowed into the Arctic Ocean by way of the Sea of Aral and the River Ob. There are remnants of the ocean life with its brackish water and unique species of seal, salmon, sturgeon, and lobsters. It has no regular tides but it does have currents that run like the Gulf Stream in determined directions. Caspian waters contain almost no oxygen, which accounts for the absence of life in its depths. Between July and September, violent storms across its surface often disrupt shipping.

* * *

During the afternoon, Svetlana and I met with a local official who gave us a brief tour of Turkmenbashi by car. The *hakeem* was in her late thirties and wore her hair up, covered by a traditional scarf. She drove us around the port facilities that were undergoing major renovation.

"The port is very important to Turkmenistan," the *hakeem* said, gently gesturing out toward the harbor. Turkmenistan accepts passenger and cargo ferry cruises from Baku and Iran. In fact, I was waiting for my Jeep to enter Turkmenistan through this port. Days before, Embassy General Services Officers said it had traveled by ship from Baltimore to Antwerp and then by rail through Europe. It was waiting at the north end of the Caspian at the Russian port of Astrakhan in what was described as a "giant traffic jam," to be shipped by barge.

"Turkmenbashi port is also important to our State oil and gas industry," we were told. I could see an oil rig was being assembled to be towed out to sea.

Krasnovodsk's port had also been the site of intrigue and a brief rebellion against the Bolsheviks in 1918. It was assisted by the British secret agent, Captain Reginald Teague-Jones, who deliberately misdirected shipments of cotton intended for the Germans during WWI. The cotton would have given the Bolsheviks much needed money to help solidify their revolution. The Teague-Jones-inspired insurrection was short lived, however, and the Captain disappeared, his fate unknown.

During WWII, when the German Army was approaching the Caucuses, some of the refinery equipment was disassembled in Baku, transported across the Caspian and reassembled here. One piece that remained of that time still displayed a USA Lend-Lease plaque.

* * *

I called Eileen from the hotel that night. At the end of the day, she had driven two hours to try to find a woman whose husband had been imprisoned for his Protestant beliefs. The young wife lived in a small district outside the capital and Eileen went to try to discuss the husband's situation. U.S.-Turkmen relations continued to be strained over Turkmenistan's harassment of minority religious faiths. It was past dark when Eileen found the wife with her two small children. With Secret Police looking on, little of substance could be discussed. Alone in her car, on her way home from her trip, a policeman waved her over. This was unusual since traffic cops seldom stopped cars with diplomatic plates. Eileen's offense was that she was driving with her lights on. She was told to turn off her lights.

* * *

The conference that brought me to Turkmenbashi was held in the windowless upstairs of a concrete block building that served as a nightclub during evening hours. The room was filled with local civic groups from the Balkan region who met to share basic information on how to manage their organizations. There were environmental groups, women's groups, health groups, and groups to help the handicapped. Late in the morning, we viewed a set of displays by junior high students who formed an ecology club that focused on cleaning the Caspian.

Simply by meeting in the open, the organizations risked

Government interference. Independent civic groups had tried to organize to help solve their own local problems but the Turkmen government continually frustrated their attempts, finding such organizations illegal.

At lunchtime, I stopped at the local bazaar to buy Eileen a birthday present—half a kilo (slightly over one pound) of black caviar for $21. There was an entire section of the bazaar where caviar sellers group together displaying sacks and sacks of the black, pasty eggs. They let customers sample from different varieties before buying.

Next to the caviar section was the meat section with its carcasses dripping blood on the concrete floor of the bazaar.

* * *

By early evening the civic conference was over. I told one participant from Ashgabat that I had managed with some effort to find a reservation on the last flight out. She gave me a look that said, "Take me with you...I don't care what it costs!" Flights in and out of Turkmenbashi were always booked. Many conference members drove the six hours from Ashgabat. Locals advised against driving at night due to the hazards of camels and other livestock that strayed onto the roads.

On the way to the airport, I rode with a cab driver who told me he had had a son born that day. I could not believe he was on duty and not at home. At the airport, I handed him a five-dollar bill.

"Dlya vashevo sinka," (for your son) I struggled to explain in Russian. It was about a week's pay for a Turkmen cab driver.

At the terminal, there was the usual scrutiny of my travel documents by a series of uniformed officials. They ushered me into an unheated holding area with a concrete floor, no seats or benches, and dim lighting. It had all the charm of a

KGB interrogation room. All was black outside. Air travel in Turkmenistan was usually when I felt the greatest potential for something to go wrong. One had to fight with disorganized mobs and surly ticket agents and submit to scrutiny by numerous Soviet-style security officials—all with the pathetic hope that you would get to travel on an aging airplane with an unknown safety record.

My examination ended without anything beyond the usual inspection. I was released to stand in a holding area with the other passengers. I met the only other identifiable Westerner, a British man who worked for a multinational logistics company. He saw the cover of my passport with the distinctive "Great Seal" of the American eagle. He introduced himself by saying with a soft British lilt, "You're a long way from home."

* * *

I walked in my front door at 10 p.m., having forgotten it was Halloween. Earlier, Charlotte went to a children's party at the Ambassador's residence dressed as a mouse. She and my wife had fallen asleep waiting for me. My daughter was still in her mouse costume.

* * *

In August of 2001, I returned to Turkmenbashi City for my third and final visit. This time I made the six-hour drive with Pavel and Anna, who worked overseeing USAID's health care projects. Anna came from an educated Russian family. Her father had been a colonel in the Soviet Army posted to Ashgabat, and her mother had been a medical doctor. Anna was a doctor trained in genetics at a prestigious Moscow university during Soviet times. She had soulful eyes, high Russian cheekbones and could flash a big smile when she was in a good mood. USAID had donated money and trained a medical staff to open a TB treatment clinic.

"The Minister of Health said he would be there," Anna

informed me the morning of our drive.

Tuberculosis is a serious health issue among Turkmen and had been a priority in our assistance for health care. Over the past 10 years, tuberculosis had reached epidemic proportions in Central Asia and exceeded 100 cases per 100,000 of population. Some segments of the Turkmen population had particularly high numbers of drug-resistant and multidrug-resistant TB cases.

* * *

During most of the route east, the road paralleled the path of the Kara Kum Canal. On the western side of the town of Goeke Teppe, I saw the hottest job in the world—road crews pouring asphalt and breaking concrete under the blaze of the desert sun. The temperature that day was somewhere over 110°F.

The Canal ended near Kyzilarvat, and with it the few fields and bits of green foliage. Adjacent to the road, were long lines of trenches as if they were half-heartedly strip-mined for gas pipelines or irrigation canals. The landscape was flat, brown plain scoured by a hot, driving wind. My eyes hurt from looking at so much brown. One theory said that the earliest humans living in jungles were most accustomed to seeing shades of green, and that this why we find green so soothing. Perhaps if I could see a mulberry tree or a few rows of cotton, my eyes would be more relaxed.

Camels meandered alongside the road and even in the road. They traveled solo or in small herds. With the exception of two albino camels, most of them were hard to see; their sand-brown coats blending in with the desert. Pavel locked the brakes at one point for a camel he had just seen, standing stock-still, straddling both lanes of road. When he honked the horn to get the beast to move, it moved toward the Suburban, reacting as if the horn was a camel call. Some miles later we drove up behind a small herd of camels walking four abreast in the middle of the road. In a most Gary-Larson-esque scene we saw five or six camels loosely congregated at a forlorn bus stop.

At the top of a rise, we looked down on a giant amphitheater of absolutely bare sand-colored hills and a cluster of buildings that was Turkmenbashi City. Beyond, the waters of the harbor and Caspian reflected the white-hot summer sky. On my first visit I had seen an industrial hell. This view was somewhat better, looking like Dante's idea for a seaside resort.

* * *

The next morning I dressed in a suit and tie for the 100-degree heat. Anna and I, and a group of USAID partners, together with local health officials, were given a tour of the new TB clinic. There were two laboratories filled with glass beakers and microscopes for testing patient samples of sputum. As TB is very infectious and can be transmitted by airborne bacteria, those who worked around it needed to be careful to wear masks and gloves.

The tour ended in a courtyard behind the clinic where the hospital staff and local officials had gathered. In the hot sun I made my remarks as brief as possible, thanking local authorities and congratulating all for establishing the clinic.

"Where is the Minister of Health?" I whispered to Anna.

"I don't know," she whispered back.

Sometimes Turkmen officials did not want to appear in public with Americans, as this might raise too high a profile. If anyone other than the President received the limelight, the officials ran the risk of being sacked for unspecified "shortcomings." President Niyazov seemed to fire half his cabinet every six months or so. I speculated that the Minister of Health was keeping his distance for this reason, despite his assurance the day before that he would attend.

Afterwards the clinic held a reception inside with offerings of cucumbers, fruit, cookies, cakes, and cola.

I turned to Anna and quietly asked, "I don't want to offend our hosts, but is it safe to eat food served in a TB clinic?"

"I think it is ok, but I would not eat the fruit," Anna said.

I followed Anna's example and took a few sips of cola and a few hard cookies.

* * *

On the way to the airport, I asked Pavel to stop at a cemetery on a rocky hilltop overlooking the airport and an oil refinery. The headstones were marked with symbols representing the person's life—usually a profession. A fishing boat was etched in the headstone for a fisherman or a truck for a truck driver, and a sewing machine and a pair of scissors for a seamstress. The saddest sight was a grave marking of a one-year-old. Carved on the child's headstone were toy balls and rattles.

Down the hill was a second cemetery for WWII Japanese POWs who had been sent here by Stalin to build Krasnovodsk's refineries. Some of the graves were marked with Japanese characters and were decorated with small shrines with framed photos of family. Their stories were unknown to me, and I tried but failed to imagine what the end of their lives must have been like—working construction under prison conditions in an arid wasteland that must have seemed like they were living in a devil's torture chamber.

Pavel pulled into the parking lot of the Turkmenbashi City Airport—the same airport that I flew out of on Halloween. What had before seemed so forbidding now looked like a benign concrete block structure. I pulled out my camera to take a picture of the terminal, and almost immediately an English-speaking Russian warned me that photographing airports was not a good idea. I could not imagine what was so sensitive about a provincial airport but remembered that cameras caused excitement here.

It was a gamble to come to the airport without a reservation. Pavel talked, then argued with every official in the airport. By the time he was finished, I think he had turned me into the most exalted dignitary on a mission of the greatest importance. Whatever he said got me on the plane and back to Ashgabat.

* * *

In a taxi ride home from the airport, I noticed a new three-story picture of the President with fireworks in the background announcing the "Golden Century" for Turkmenistan. This billboard faced a five-story billboard of the President, as a bust floating among the clouds with a blue sky.

We passed through one neighborhood where an Embassy colleague formerly lived. Her house was now a pile of rubble. Following the pattern of all-powerful autocrats, the President had also decided to remake the capitol. The neighborhood was one of many that had been leveled to build six-lane boulevards suitable for military parades. The colleague had come home one day to find bulldozers outside her house. A few months ago, Eileen, Charlotte and I had been invited to the colleague's home, where we enjoyed good conversation and a home-cooked dinner. Today, scavengers picked through the debris looking to salvage scraps of metal plumbing and wiring.

The cab let me out at the compound gates. The intense heat had broken, and a soft breeze had stirred up. The white sky had turned blue with small wisps of clouds and the moon rose in the eastern sky. The sun's path had taken it down to an escarpment at the far edge of Kopet Dag, illuminating the folds and crevices behind the compound. This was what photographers call the "golden hour."

JOURNEY 9

Taliban Neighbor

You can't appreciate home 'til you've left it... nor Old Glory 'til you see it hanging on a brown stick on the shanty of a consul in a foreign town.

--O.Henry

After the horror of the September 11th attacks, the most beautiful sight was a big, gray U.S. Air Force C-17 cargo plane. It sat a mile from the Turkmenbashi Airport Terminal at the end of the runway like a dinosaur at rest, waiting to be greeted. The plane did not have the sleek lines of a fighter, nor did it bristle with weaponry, but it had a small American flag on the tail fin and black lettering "United States of America" along the side.

A month earlier, next door neighbor Afghanistan had become the focus of America's military response. Osama bin Laden and his Al Qaeda forces had been treated as "guests" of the Taliban, and used the country as a base of operations for terrorist attacks. The U.S. Embassy in Ashgabat was a small outpost of America in a country with a 750-mile open border with Afghanistan. Our initial anxiety was due to simply not knowing what would happen next. Some locals now passed rumors that Taliban were on the streets of Ashgabat.

Although Turkmenistan had been one of the only countries that had relations with the Taliban, the American Government clearly wanted Turkmenistan's support in fighting this new threat that lay next door. The Taliban had already issued an ominous edict that any country to provide assistance to the United State risked being attacked. The C-17 was a small reminder that America remembered that a few of its own were out here at the edge of this new war. It was nice to know that even here—in a country most Americans could not find on a map—an American plane could land and we would not be left behind.

The crew emerged from the plane with some bewilderment and hesitation. When I approached, I had to yell to be heard over the roar of the four jet engines.

"John Kropf ...American Embassy! Welcome to Ashgabat!" I shouted. Hearing myself, it sounded like I was reading from the script of a bad movie.

The pilot's expression turned to one of recognition and some relief, as if he had not been completely sure where he was, but my presence confirmed he had landed at the right destination. I pointed to the Kopet Dag Mountains to the south, and he was amazed to see how close they were to Iran.

His plane, for the moment, was the most advanced piece of military equipment in all of Turkmenistan. The crew had started from an Air Force base in Charleston, South Carolina, and had picked up pallets of blankets, tents, medical kits and high-energy biscuits in Italy. The supplies were lashed down in the hold with cargo netting. It was the first load of humanitarian aid for the Afghans who had been displaced from their homes as a result of drought and the U.S. war against the Taliban.

The pilot, Steve, had been laid off from one of the major U.S. airlines following September 11th and had been activated with the South Carolina Air National Guard. They would be returning home to the United States after a night's rest.

We watched as Steve's crew used its own forklift to unload pallets of shrink-wrapped supplies from the plane's hold and parked them on the tarmac. A convoy of waiting trucks from one of the Non-Governmental Organizations (NGOs) waited to deliver the supplies into Afghanistan. Steve invited me into the plane for an inspection, an ice cold Coke and a slice of pizza left over from their last refueling stop in Sicily. For a moment I considered asking him for a ride home.

* * *

Like in the United States the morning of September 11th, everything in Turkmenistan had seemed normal that day. The weather was especially nice, with blue sky and seasonal breezes. The only unusual thing was how quiet it was at the Embassy. We had been in-between Ambassadors; waiting for our new Ambassador to be confirmed by the Senate. In the interim, the Embassy was lead by a *Charge de Affaires*, essentially the Deputy of the Embassy working in an acting Ambassador capacity. The *Charge* was out of the country for the day on official business, leaving the third ranking official of the Embassy in charge. That official happened to be Eileen. Eileen had quietly worked through the day and was happy it was drawing to a close.

It was almost six o'clock in the evening when Eileen and I returned home to the compound. I had arrived a few minutes before and was putting on a *Little Bear* video for Charlotte. I paused to watch a moment of CNN. The compound's satellite dish allowed us to have at least minimal access to western news channels. With the time difference, it was a about nine a.m. Eastern Daylight Time. CNN showed the first tower of the World Trade Center burning from a crash by a passenger plane. While I was still trying to sort out how this had happened, a second plane flashed across the screen, like a black crow disappearing behind the other tower. Plumes of flaming jet fuel erupted from the other side of the building.

I heard Eileen in the doorway outside saying to a colleague, "Thank God nothing happened today."

For the next hour the news reported scraps of information and rumors. News clips showed President Bush departing hurriedly after reading a story to school children in Florida; the footage of the airplane crashes was repeated again and again; this abruptly changed to a camera shot in Washington, D.C. showing a plume of black smoke from somewhere behind the old Executive Office Building. Reporters could not identify its source. The White House was evacuated. The U.S. Capitol was evacuated. There were reports but no camera shots that the Pentagon had smoke coming from it. Another hijacked plane was unaccounted for. The Pentagon had been hit with a plane. The President flew to an Air Force base in Louisiana. There was a plane crash in southwestern Pennsylvania. A car bomb was reported at the Department of State. The lack of pattern to the attacks left us wondering what would be the next target.

By evening's end, the *Charge* was back in the country. Most of the families on the compound had gathered in our living room to watch CNN. Watching the disintegration of World Trade Center towers from the other side of the globe seemed unreal. The catastrophe was the Pearl Harbor equivalent for this generation of Americans who watched it live.

For the next two days, the Embassy was closed to the public. Our local employees were kept at home, and our own movements on and off the compound were limited. This was when living on a compound seemed to pose more of a risk than a measure of security. Here were all the Americans collected together in one open and identifiable location instead of dispersed throughout the city. We were an easy target. The Embassy's security officer and the six-man Marine Security Guard Detachment had been alerted. Months before, I had bought several t-shirts from the Marines. The shirts showed a map of Turkmenistan bordered by Afghanistan, Iran, and Uzbekistan with the caption, "Surrounded by Danger—we got 'em right where we want 'em." Now the words took on a deeper meaning.

On September 12th, the Turkmen government TV took the unprecedented step of breaking from its highly predictable pattern of news stories devoted to the President and instead showed the attack as the first story with about ten minutes of coverage. In the following days, coverage reverted to the Turkmen President's achievements and the cotton harvest. Even the CNN segment Turkmen TV showed as part of its world news reported nothing relevant to the disaster and instead showed segments on the slowdown of Mazda exports from Japan and a second story on modern African music performers.

Life on the streets of Ashgabat seemed eerily unchanged: motorists still drove their cars haphazardly, traffic cops still indiscriminately waved over drivers, old women still swept the streets with brooms of bundled twigs. The capital city's four-page daily newspaper, *Neutral Turkmenistan*, focused on the cotton harvest and preparations for the country's Tenth Anniversary celebration. The paper featured a new daily portrait of the President leaning forward, one arm over the desk like an avuncular talk show host.

Even with the limited Government information about the tragedy, it was clear the Turkmen people found outside sources for their news. Hundreds of bouquets of flowers were left as offerings of condolence along the front fence of the Embassy. It created a colorful stripe down the sidewalk and was a touching gesture for the usually reserved Turkmen and Russian inhabitants of Ashgabat. At a memorial service hosted by the Vatican Embassy, everyone treated the small group of Americans like bereaved family members at a funeral.

There were less than 200 Americans in the country, including Peace Corps volunteers. We were on foreign soil in a place not many Americans knew existed. The combination of factors made the tragedy seem more intense to our small group. The atmosphere at the Embassy was one of sober concentration.

After two days of a closed office, I returned to work to find my small office staff had erected a makeshift shrine in our conference room with a pencil and penholder, holding a small American flag and two candles. There was a card of sympathy. The staff looked to me, wondering if I had been personally affected by the tragedy. I gathered them together and gave some impromptu remarks to express my appreciation and assure them that all was safe at the office.

From my office window, I had a good vantage point to judge the mood of the landscape. A line of low-hanging rain clouds obscured the peaks of the Kopet Dag. To the north, towering, ashen-colored cumulous clouds loomed, dwarfing the city as if representing the apocalypse approaching from the vast wastelands of the Kara Kum.

In the outside world, things did not continue as before. American coverage discussed Turkmenistan as a front-line state in what the media called the "first war of the 21st Century." Americans were introduced to Turkmenistan on September 12th, 2001, when network news anchors displayed giant "war room" maps of Afghanistan and its neighbors. In some cases, the introduction was misleading. FOX News labeled it "Uzbekistan" for the first two days of its coverage. Friends and relatives who never looked at Turkmenistan on a map suddenly sent e-mails saying they never realized exactly where it was. They asked when we were coming home.

Within days, the Embassy issued a travel warning advising Americans against travel to Turkmenistan; Peace Corps volunteers were withdrawn and put on planes back to the States; and some of USAID's partners pulled out their American employees.

Most dramatic for me was that the U.S. Government had begun a process of authorized departure that allowed some Embassy employees and dependents to return to the States. Eileen decided that she and Charlotte would leave first and that I would follow sometime later.

October 1st, at one o'clock in the morning, I saw Eileen carrying a sleeping Charlotte out to a small, white van that would take them to the Airbus and back to the United States. It was an empty feeling. We had all arrived in the middle of the night and now two of the three of us were leaving the same way. The two figures disappeared behind the doors of the van that drove toward the Lufthansa plane.

* * *

That night, the wind blew with more than normal ferocity. In the morning, I discovered a window in the Jeep was open a crack, which had allowed wind to cover everything with fine silt. The earthy smell of Turkmenistan permeated the car. Fine sand clung to the steering wheel, the gearshift, everything I touched. I was absorbing Turkmenistan every time I drove my car.

I stopped at one of the hotels designated for foreigners to meet a UN colleague. In the hotel driveway were three large Toyota land cruisers with license plates in Arabic numerals. There had been rumors of Taliban and Al Qaeda being spotted in hotels. Now I wondered was there any truth to them. The UN colleague, who lived at the hotel, came out to meet me. When I mentioned the cars to her, she explained that it was normal. They belonged to Arabs from Gulf States who came to Turkmenistan every year to do falconry out in the Kara Kum. The valuable birds sat blindfolded on special perches in their master's hotel rooms.

On October 5th, our new Ambassador arrived. Ambassador Laura Kennedy was energetic and had experience in the Former Soviet Union and Turkey. This was her first assignment as Ambassador. The crises had accelerated her arrival. Weeks before, she was among a group of Ambassador nominees waiting for Senate approval. After September 11th, the Senate and the State Department must have collectively looked at a map, realized the strategic importance of Turkmenistan, and the fact that we did not yet have an Ambassador over there.

The next day, U.S. Air Force and Navy planes began bombing targets in Afghanistan. The third night was reported as some of the heaviest bombing. I lay awake in bed thinking that in nearby skies our pilots were in pressurized flight suits, stealthily flying their machines over desert landscape to their targets.

* * *

Despite the military drama unfolding just over the horizon, activity in Ashgabat continued to be focused on Turkmenistan's 10th Anniversary celebration. In preparation for the Independence Day parade, soldiers with AK-47s practiced rectangular formations in the Presidential square and the Olympic-sized stadium across the street from USAID's office. At night, government buildings were trimmed in colored neon lights, giving the city a continuous holiday feel. From a distance, it was if the city was an outline for an art deco style cartoon.

Construction on a 10th Anniversary Monument—a fountain with ten larger-than-life Ahal-Tekke horses—continued around the clock, even under floodlights at night. South of the city, high-rise buildings were being constructed at a record pace. At night, their construction crews worked under floodlights. The workers' hammering and clanging easily carried across the flat desert and reverberated in the compound. It seemed odd that the Government should be in such a hurry to build them, since dozens of other newly constructed buildings stood empty.

The abrupt transitions could be jarring. Where months ago there had been patches of desert—a landscape more suitable to nomadic tribes in yurts—high-rise buildings in white marble now stood. There had been no gradual transitions with sidewalks, shops, or a surrounding neighborhood. A site would be cleared, cranes erected, and 24-story buildings were constructed. President Niyazov seemed to want to be the George Washington of Turkmenistan without waiting. He wanted all the monuments and buildings of a capital city in his lifetime.

Ashgabat otherwise maintained a sense of surreal normalcy. Turkmen Television's morning programming showed a military uniformed presenter greeting viewers with a poem. A patriotic song was performed over footage of the Turkmen military. A second segment showed soldiers at the Turkmenbashi Military Institute taking an oath by placing one hand on a light machine gun, followed by footage of soldiers being interviewed, and then demonstrating hand-to-hand fighting. That night, I saw a grainy old Tom and Jerry cartoon dubbed into Turkmen.

The only outward sign of anything different was when I was stopped by KNB and two plain-clothes officers from the Ministry of Interior at Mir Bazaar while buying apples. They asked to see my passport, which I showed them and which they only briefly examined. They apologized for the inconvenience and sent me on my way. I saw they stopped another man—an Iranian-looking gentleman with a button-up collarless shirt and a beard. The common thread seemed to be the beard (I had grown a beard by this time). Turkmen authorities seemed to be taking some steps to patrol their

own country by profiling men with beards. They were looking for Afghans or Iranians who may have overstayed their
visas.

While Turkmenistan continued with its anniversary preparations and life as normal, Western media and relief workers
were desperately trying to enter the country. As a neighbor
to Afghanistan, the media wanted to use Turkmenistan as an
alternate route into the war zone. Foreign journalists, including the BBC, were denied entry visas. Despite intense worldwide attention on Central Asia, Turkmenistan remained suspicious of foreigners, keeping the rest of the planet at arm's
length. About this time I noticed one of the few articles that
I had ever seen about Turkmenistan. An article in *The New
York Times* described President Niyazov as a "dictator at the
center of one of the world's most bizarre personality cults
[who] views himself as a demigod and has ordered that his
image adorn every coin and bank note and that it be displayed in every public space." Accurate or not, it should have
come as no surprise that the Turkmen government did not
welcome foreign journalists with open arms. Freedom of the
press was not something recognized here.

The relief workers fared only slightly better. As American
employees for USAID's partners had left at the end of September, relief workers displaced from Afghanistan looked to
find a way in. They either were thrown out of Afghanistan
by the Taliban or evacuated because of fear for their personal safety. One enterprising group closed its field office
in Afghanistan and flew themselves to Pakistan. From there
they flew to the UAE, where they finally got tourist visas to
Ashgabat. Turkmenistan's location was the draw. From here,
they planned to work with USAID and the UN to deliver
relief supplies to the Afghans, and once the fighting died
down, return to Afghanistan.

Keenly aware of UN estimates that as many as 50,000 Af-

ghan refugees might be displaced and move into Turkmenistan, we were in a wait-and-see mode. However, most of our
discussions with the Government to assist in relief efforts
ground to a halt and every office was occupied with preparing for the celebrations.

* * *

Each time I talked with Eileen, we discussed my return.
Eileen and Charlotte were living with Eileen's parents in the
safety of western Massachusetts. Turkmenistan's location as
a relief corridor was becoming increasingly important. I felt
immediacy with my job that I had not known before. It was
a change in perspective. In Washington, I was used to sitting behind a desk giving legal analysis to issues that often
seemed abstract and distant from some real-world cause and
effect. It was much harder to recognize the results of my
work, which often took months to unfold. In Ashgabat, I was
at a small outpost in a remote location representing an organization that was in the business of providing assistance. A
war had started next door. USAID and relief organizations
needed someone on the ground to help organize the effort.
The idea of putting food in the hands of a family that was
hungry was very tangible and very immediate and unlike
anything I had worked on in Washington.

Eileen understood the feeling. She had served in a small
consulate in Dubai during the Gulf War assisting Americans.
She wanted me to come home but recognized the importance of staying. The combination of factors worked to pull
me in different directions. Every day I looked at Charlotte's
small handprint smeared on one of the glass doors and could
not bring myself to wash it off. At the same time, I felt the
urge to stay. How many chances to really help somebody
does one have, I kept asking myself. As the weeks passed,
we inched toward the decision that I should stay as long as
necessary.

After I decided to stay on, my diet took a strange twist. Our pantry had a supply of dry food and canned goods that we had stocked up to feed a family of three for a year. For meals I would sometimes peel open kid-sized fruit cups of peaches and pears and knock them back in one gulp as if I was doing whiskey shots. Other days I would eat Wheat-a-Bix for breakfast and dinner because we still had a couple dozen boxes left. My biggest concern was rationing coffee enough to last until Christmas when I hoped to make a visit home.

* * *

As the Tenth Anniversary drew closer, accomplishments were being celebrated daily. Driving to work one morning, the mile-long road to the newly constructed Turkmenbashi hospital was lined with doctors and nurses and other medical staff in white lab coats and tall hats that looked like chefs' hats. The President was expected to open the hospital that morning.

The road along Turkmenbashi Street was lined with booths decorated with green, white, and yellow crepe tablecloths and balloons. One near Turkmen State University had plastic tables and chairs, making an impromptu café. The vendors sold Coke, Fanta, Sprite, candy, and baked goods—the same goods as you could buy in the bazaars. I could not help but feel the celebration was slightly tragic as a light drizzle fell, dampening the crepe paper.

The evening news reported the President had been granted his fourth Hero of Turkmenistan award, even though he had continuously refused to take another hero award. The National Council also decided to confer on him the rank of Field Marshall—promoting him from General of the Army.

The same gray clouds and drizzle continued through the two days of parades and celebrations. On the final night, fireworks were shot into the damp sky from all over the city.

* * *

We had heard the UN's prediction that the war would push refugees into Afghanistan's neighboring countries. Part of USAID's mission was to give assistance to any refugees. Finally, with the help of the Turkmen government, we went looking for refugees.

We would be riding in a Soviet-made helicopter that had likely seen service during the Soviet-Afghan war. Minutes before leaving for the airport, I was overtaken with anxiety. Was the helicopter short some critical spare part? What if American fighters mistook us for a Taliban helicopter? Weeks before, U.S. forces had shot down one of our own Black Hawk helicopters in Afghanistan in a friendly fire incident. I wrote an "if-something-should-happen" letter to Charlotte, now three years old. I tried to tell her everything she might want to know about me and what advice I thought she might need—all in the span of five minutes.

Our Embassy group flew to a helicopter base in Mary that had been used as a staging ground during the Soviet-Afghan war. We were directed to a helicopter that looked as if it was a giant bloated insect and had been painted in a mixed desert camouflage. It was parked along with a couple of dozen others that had had their rotors removed. I looked twice to make sure the rotors had not been left off of ours.

Inside were bench seats with two 100-gallon auxiliary tanks on either side. I thought to myself, "Yes, please—take all the fuel you need. Don't want to get caught short near the Afghan border." The windows looked like portholes that had been removed from a ship.

On takeoff, the intense noise, vibration and smell of aviation fuel combined to start an immediate headache. "Only a couple more hours of this," I thought.

We flew east in the direction of Afghanistan. The landscape was a flat, arid waste covered by a dirty white sky heavy with heat and sand. Dusty hills rolled away into the horizon. There were no signs of refugees. The land formed a natural barrier that seemed incompatible with human survival. Occasionally in the middle of this vastness I saw a shepherd herding a flock of black-haired sheep.

We landed at Gushgy, the southernmost point in Turkmenistan. Our hosts drove us through the small town, past a whitewashed Russian orthodox cross on a hilltop that Tzar Nicholas had ordered to mark the southernmost point in the Russian empire.

At Gushgy's border checkpoint we looked across two red and white wooden gates into a small cluster of buildings that was the village of Turgundi in Afghanistan. An irregular ridgeline of tan mountains loomed in the background. A set of train tracks, a branch line from Mary of the Trans-Caspian Railroad, ended about half a mile inside the border. It was all strangely quiet. There was no activity to been seen on the Afghan side of the border. Somewhere over the ridgeline, 80 miles down the road, was Heart, where some of the heaviest bombing had taken place. American and Northern Alliance forces were fighting the Taliban and Al Qaeda. It was a drama that we could only imagine.

We flew along the Afghan border before banking west toward Mary. The terrain was beautiful in its rugged desolation. On the Turkmen side were several patches of wild pistachio trees. As I looked into Afghanistan, the smooth undulating hills looked like an ocean of brown swells and troughs. If someone wanted to hide, never to be found, this seemed like the place to do it.

* * *

By November, NGOs were finally able to get some workers into Turkmenistan, thanks in a large part to substantial U.S. lobbying. USAID had also sent out a special disaster team to help organize shipping non-food items including plastic sheeting, tents, wool blanket, and coats. The World Food Program came equipped with people and money. Finally, the first of many humanitarian flights to deliver aid by way of Turkmenistan started in November.

A "humanitarian mercenary" was how Simon, one red-bearded American, described himself. The combination of his small frame and bushy red beard gave him the initial appearance of an oversized Leprechaun with a serious demeanor. The first time we met, he had been living in Afghanistan and grew the beard in an attempt to minimize scrutiny of the Taliban, who had issued edicts that men not shave their facial hair. I thought about the futility of a red-bearded man trying not to stand out in a world of black beards. Two days ago, Simon had been expelled by the Taliban and found his way to Turkmenistan by way of Pakistan.

Simon had pursued a doctorate in American literature at Columbia University only two years ago. He had decided to change the course of his life with relief work, a decision similar to what I imagined men who joined the French Foreign Legion used to do. Talking to him, I sensed that a certain adrenaline rush came from helping people in desperate situations. It was a high that could become addictive.

The next time I saw him, he had shaved his beard. In the coming weeks, he organized relief convoys of hundreds of trucks that carried blankets, tents, food, and medical supplies. The Afghan truck drivers and scores of day laborers that loaded the supplies by hand had become his army of humanitarian mercenaries.

During October and November, USAID bought tons of relief supplies, and Simon was indispensable with organizing the hand-off of those supplies that were then shipped via hundreds of trucks. They drove more than two hundred miles over horribly rutted tracks in the desert to the Afghan border. Because there were not news media here, the outside world did not know of this extraordinary effort.

Events moved quickly. The Northern Alliance forces now controlled the upper half of Afghanistan, including areas along the Turkmen and Uzbek borders. In the first week of November, six C-17's from McGuire Air Force Base in Washington state landed with humanitarian relief—food and non-food items. The head of USAID was on hand to witness Simon's humanitarian mercenary skills at work. As Ambassador Kennedy, the head of USAID, Andrew Natsios, and numerous Turkmen government officials came to the airport to mark the occasion, Simon called trucks in by walkie-talkies.

"OK-Now," was the only instruction he needed to give. Moments later, trucks began driving across the tarmac and queuing up to receive pallets of supplies.

In December, during the month of Ramadan, President Bush personally saw off two American Red Cross humanitarian flights. The first C-17s carried over 1,600 winter jackets, 1,500 winterized family-size tents, and 10,000 gift parcels of clothes, school supplies, and candies for children of Afghanistan. American school children had funded the donations.

* * *

I saw Simon and many of the relief workers together in the week before Christmas. They had gathered together for a last supper at a hotel with Turkmenistan's only Italian chef. The relief workers were a culture unto themselves. They were a diverse group of Americans and Europeans who knew each other from previous disasters. Many had worked overseas for years, as if they knew no other life. They recognized each other with a carefree camaraderie: "Were you in the Congo? Or was it Kosovo?" If they did not know each other they usually knew the same people. The supper was the last time I would see Simon in Turkmenistan. He and the other relief workers disappeared as suddenly as they had come. All were going separate ways back to Afghanistan, some via Europe to spend a short Christmas holiday.

By Christmas, Turkmenistan became a leading aid corridor to Afghanistan. Second to Pakistan, Turkmenistan's land corridor delivered over a third of the American aid to Afghanistan. While some expected aid would flow from Uzbekistan across the "Friendship Bridge" at Termez, Uzbekistan—the same bridge Soviet tanks and troop carriers had crossed when they invaded Afghanistan thirty years ago—Uzbek authorities frustrated attempts by international relief groups to use this route. As a result, only a trickle of the humanitarian aid was able to travel through Uzbekistan. Turkmenistan's position had proved vital.

After a brief trip home for the holidays, my return into Turkmenistan was difficult. In two weeks, I had bonded with my family and became reaquainted with western comforts, privacy, and freedoms. On the return flight on Uzbek Airlines, I felt like an agent of Santa Claus. I bought the largest duffle bag I could find at a camping supply store and loaded it with Barbie dolls, over-the-counter medicines, cosmetics, coffee, and even a fuel pump for my Jeep (which died the day I left). I barely had room for clothes.

It was now January and most of the aid workers had gone. The Taliban had been routed. With U.S. funding, the World Food Program had brought thousands of tons of wheat to Turkmenistan by train and was bagging it and trucking it in from Turkmenibad. By spring, Peace Corps volunteers returned. The anxiousness of the fall and winter months dissipated. I could turn back to regular work in Turkmenistan and think about going home in a few months.

UNKNOWN SANDS

JOURNEY 10

Home by Way of Dinosaur Tracks

Leaving a country is like dying: we leave a world for an indefinite future.

--Peregrine Hodson, Under a Sickle Moon

At least one travel writer has written that leaving a country is like dying: we leave one world for the indefinite future of another. I understand this. When you realize your own mortality, you want to leave some mark in this world so those you leave behind may remember you. Likewise, when I travel from a place where I've lived, I want to make sure that the place leaves its mark on me—that I not forget what I learned there.

For nearly two years, I worked for USAID in Central Asia's most remote country. The closer I came to leaving, the more I wanted to make my mark on Turkmenistan.

The month before I left, I made ambitious plans to travel around the country as much as I could, looking for opportunities to leave a lasting, positive mark. I assigned myself to check up on the construction of a small school for Tajik refugees outside the town of Kerki, located in Turkmenistan's most eastern province of Lebop that bordered the Afghan frontier. Tucked away in the far eastern corner of the same province was the remote mountain village of Khodja Pil Ata, where USAID had made a grant to buy a personal computer for the community. The village was in a rugged area called Kugatang that contained the world's longest set of dinosaur tracks. Kugatang was an isolated, mountainous region in a far corner of the country, bordered by Uzbekistan and Afghanistan. It sat alone on the northeastern side of the Amudarya River that by rights of natural geography should have been in Uzbekistan.

This was USAID's smallest grant in the country's most remote area. The villagers of Khodja Pil Ata seldom had visitors from the outside. I decided to see the computer and the tracks for myself. By an odd logic, I thought the more remote the location, the better chance I had at leaving a mark.

* * *

The first leg of the trip was by plane from Turkmenistan's capital, Ashgabat, to the provincial city of Turkmenibad. Pavel and Jamala would be waiting in Turkmenibad with our office's only vehicle.

At the Ashgabat airport, the passengers milled around the departure gate. Even with my poor Russian, I could overhear that the topic of conversation ahead of me was whether we would be flying one of the usual Soviet-era Yak-40's or one of the recently purchased brand new Boeing 717's. A tan-skinned Turkmen wearing a black canvas coat and short *tilpek* looked back at me and, seeing me as a westerner, gestured a thumbs up with the words, "Boeing the best." There seemed to be smiles all around that we would be traveling on the Boeing.

While I suppose we might have had a lot of different opinions about politics or the proper role for the United States in world affairs, in matters of immediate personal safety, like trusting your life to aircraft technology, all disagreements instantly evaporated. U.S. technology was the unanimous favorite. I smiled and managed to reply, "Boeing Khorosho." (Boeing Good.)

On the tarmac, we were directed to a Soviet Tu-144. There was an audible sigh of disappointment.

* * *

The flight to Turkmenibad lasted about an hour. My in flight reading was a copy of the four-page daily newspaper, *Neutral Turkmenistan.* The day's headlines consisted of:

"President Receives Letters of Congratulation from World Leaders for Turkmenistan's National Flag Day"

"New Gas Compressor Station Opened"

"Wheat Harvest Figures (ahead of last year)"

"Ministry of Agriculture Purchases New Tractors"

* * *

In Turkmenibad, the sky was a crisp blue with a slight breeze. Pavel and Jamal were waiting with the Suburban. Pavel's English had developed much faster than my Russian.

"Sir, I have prepared the super bun for our mountain drive."

"The what?"

"The SUPER BUN," he said louder and more emphatically in his Russian accent.

"That's good," I said feigning confidence but still having no idea what he was talking about. Only when we walked to our vehicle and I saw the words "Chevrolet Suburban" did I understand what Pavel's truncated pronunciation of "Super Bun" meant.

Pavel's enthusiasm for new English words outpaced my comprehension. He liked American slang and kept a pocket-sized dictionary of American slang by his side in the Suburban.

"Sir, our mechanic I think he is fleecing us," Pavel warned.

This was unwelcome news since we were about to drive remote mountain roads. I promised to look into it as soon as we got back to Ashgabat.

From Turkmenibad, we drove two-and-half hours to the small town of Atamurat, the last town before Afghanistan.

Because of the proximity to Afghanistan, Turkmen authorities set up a checkpoint about 6 miles outside of town. We stopped in front of a guardhouse as two border security officials came over to the car to inspect our papers. I needed to show my two special permissions necessary to travel in the region: one from the Ministry of Foreign Affairs and one from the Ministry of Nature Protection. Behind us, a giant Soviet-made dump truck rattled to a stop. With a broken hood latch and smashed headlamps, it towered over the Suburban, loudly idling with a strange noise like a combination of electrical shorts and grinding gears.

After half an hour of uniformed officials checking our passports and studying my permissions, we were waved through.

East of Atamurat, the scenery was dull, brown, and flat. After almost two years, I was learning that there were different degrees of flat desert landscape, much the way the Inuits were said to see snow. I was learning to see the slight differences in the arid wastes of Turkmenistan. Occasionally there was a solitary figure squatting along the roadside with nothing and no one in sight for miles. I tried to guess whether these individuals were waiting for something or just being alone with their thoughts because there was nothing else.

Late in the afternoon, after another checkpoint, we crossed the Amudarya's meandering brown waters on a makeshift pontoon bridge. We were upstream from where Alexander the Great had crossed it over two millennia ago when it represented the outer limits of the known western world. Now, the River wandered around sandbanks in the middle of the channel without much authority. I was disappointed, expecting something greater from this body of water considering the impressive historical association.

* * *

With the Amudarya several hours behind us, we drove along a one-lane gravel road into the village of Khodja Pil Ata. Our route had made a steady climb out of the high desert and into green hills. Up in the hills, we entered a cloud of misting rain.

We were hours late and the people in the village had been awaiting the arrival of "the American" all day. One of the local farmers had donated a sheep to be slaughtered in honor of my visit.

The *Archena*, a deputy mayor of sorts, greeted us. She had long, gray hair worn up with a headscarf. I guessed she was in her late sixties, but in the dark of the rainy night, I could have been off ten years either way. She led our small group to her house in steady formal movements as a society hostess would escort us into an elegant dinner party.

Everyone removed their shoes in the traditional Turkmen style and stepped into the rear doorway of her home. Our pile of shoes looked like pairs of tired reptiles at rest. I was seated on the floor covered with room-sized Ersari tribal rugs and served green tea and fish soup. The *Archena* said the sheep could still be slaughtered.

"I appreciate the honor but I feel I can't do your hospitality justice at this hour," I said with Jamala translating my words into Turkmen. "I couldn't give the occasion its due."

I was offered a plate of giant Mushrooms called *Kozskura* meaning "sheep's buttocks" because they resembled the white flanks of the local breed of sheep.

More courses of food were presented and we began to talk about life in Kugatang.

"I am in charge of women's health, children's issues, and

culture," the *Archena* began with Jamala translating.

During Soviet times these had been traditional respon-
sibilities for local women leaders. We were only 125 miles
from Dushanbe, the capital of Tajikistan, and 800 miles from
Ashgabat—as far away from the capital as one could travel
and still be in the country. The influences seemed closer to
Uzbek or Tajik than Turkmen. The men wore long cotton
robes of blue or green. Women wore *ikat* silk robes of the
type seen more frequently in Uzbekistan. I could not help
but think she was now uncertain of her current responsi-
bilities and found herself at a loss with the changes that had
come from Ashgabat since independence.

"During Soviet days," she said, "the town received a lot of
attention and was a popular location for summer holidays.
They called us 'Little Switzerland' because of our green
mountains in the spring." There was a slight wistfulness to
her voice.

The green in the hills was fleeting; much like the ephemeral nature of the cherry trees at the Washington Tidal Basin
are remembered year round for their brief display of wispy,
pink blossoms.

"You are here at the right time," she said.

Even though we had approached the town at twilight,
we had been able make out lush green trees and flowering
shrubs. Soon the green would wither away and the mountains would take on their dust brown color, which marked
them for most of the year. Kugatang was considered a mi-
cro-environmental zone. It had its own climate and growing seasons distinct from the rest of Turkmenistan. Apricots,
apples, and cherries grew in its valleys and hillsides.

Despite the hour and the fact that I had dozed off during
part of the *Archena's* welcoming dinner, we had to visit "the
computer." It was the pride of the town government. There
would be no time to see it tomorrow. Our group trooped to

a simple one floor concrete building. The *Archena* unlocked its doors and showed me into a special room where it was kept.

"The machine is used everyday to create birth, death, and health records for the village," she explained. "If someone from Kugatang needs an official letter, they come here to have it typed." The building was also where the village had its only telephone.

The *Archena* had brought with her a young woman who had been specially designated as its operator. She booted up the PC to show that it was in working condition.

The computer's effect must have been similar to the effect the first television had when it appeared in American small towns. The *Archena* expressed pride in the service it provided for the community.

That night we slept in a drafty and dilapidated dormitory that was part of a sanitarium. Ten years ago the dormitory might have been filled with tourists from around the Soviet Union. Now Kugatang was forgotten and off-limits because of it was part of a sensitive border region. It received few tourists. I fell asleep inhaling drafts of cold, aromatic mountain air.

Morning in Kugatang brought a steady rain. This would turn the mountain roads into slurry.

The *Archena* had assigned us a local guide, Guvanch, to find the dinosaur tracks. He was a quiet, impassive man who had seen the tracks before. He rode in the front seat next to Pavel.

The road was deeply rutted and made worse by the rain. Pavel had turned back on a prior trip with Larry because of difficult road conditions and he was now determined to show that he could make the drive. If the Suburban had gotten stuck or plunged over the side, any effective help would have been days off.

The mud road led into green valleys surrounded by deep rust-colored hills, tinted by their heavy iron content. The craggy green hills and mist looked more like the rocky glens of a "Little Scotland" than the alpine mountain valleys of Switzerland. We were the lone vehicle in the valley.

The further we drove, the more prehistoric the landscape appeared. The valley floor was dotted with yellow plants. They looked like giant stalks of yellow broccoli.

"They are good for stomach or digestive problems," said Atamurat.

Guvanch guided us to stop at what I called "Caveman Rock."

It was a rust-colored boulder, nearly a perfect sphere and the size of an overblown beach ball. The rock marked a gravesite.

"Local legend," said Guvanch, "is that a strongman carried the heavy boulder into the valley to prove his great strength. He died near this spot and was buried."

From that day on, his challenge was for all comers to try to move it. I imagined a Neanderthal in animal skins pounding his chest, bellowing and carrying the rock around as a show of prowess to other cavemen.

In a show of manliness, Pavel attempted to move it. He bent down, embraced the boulder and twisted his face into a mock grimace of pain. The boulder did not move.

"Pavel, lift with your legs!" I encouraged. He grimaced more but then released his grip with an expression of exasperation. He stood up and waved his hands at the rock in disgust as if he had been silly to waste his time with the whole stunt.

Atamurat guided us to the next stop only a few miles down the trail. He pointed out the "Medusa" fossil that was at the foot of a large outcrop. After several million years, it showed itself in well-defined relief as a giant shell. Covering just a quarter of a mile, we had traveled several million years from cavemen to invertebrate. The Medusa looked like a giant coil of rope petrified in rock.

Onward. The trail climbed a ridge looking into the last valley. Jamala could see I was trying to take notes on a steno pad while being wildly bounced around the back seat.

"John is our Marco Polo for Kugatang," she said to the rest of the car. (When I tried to read my notes later, ninety percent of them were illegible.)

Opposite to our position on the ridge we could see a stream of water gushing from a mountain wall. The mountaintop above was marked with a white, ragged banner on a stick and other bits of cloth flying around it like small kites that had their lines caught in the rocks. The marking meant the stream was sacred. Like other streams I had seen in the Kopet Dag Mountains in the south of the country, the Turkmen maintained ancient pre-Islamic nature cults. There was a reverence for the elements of water, earth, and fire that still inspired local people to erect such markers.

Road conditions deteriorated to a dangerous point where the route was just slurry and deep ruts. When the Suburban bogged down in a rut, I would grit my teeth hoping its Detroit-made four-wheel drive was enough for the crude mountainside. Three or four times I cursed loudly out of anxiety as if I had been suddenly struck with Tourette's syndrome. Jamala told me to calm myself because I was disturbing Pavel's confidence.

* * *

We parked in a muddy field at the base of a mountainside where there was crude farm and followed a rough trail up into rocks and boulders. A steady rain saturated us. After about an hour of hiking on slippery rock and mud, we arrived on a smooth shale hillside. What stretched before us looked like a giant cement sidewalk that someone had walked on before it was dry. We were looking out at the world's longest set of dinosaur tracks. Each footprint was about the size of a waiter's serving platter.

"The shoe size was about 94, quintuple E width," I said to Jamala.

The prints showed three distinct claws that dug into the earth. Pavel and I walked over and posed with our shoes on other side of the first print. Even in our clunky hiking boots, our feet looked puny in comparison. The track led in a steady direction up the mountainside. Paleontologist Martin Lockley, who had been part of a National Geographic expedition to study the tracks in 1995, estimated that the beast was traveling about 4 miles per hour.

We occupied the same space as this monster. Millions of years ago, it might have been a similar rainy day on earth. The soil must have been muddy enough from rainstorms for the behemoth to sink in. Footprints were normally ephemeral things. They showed that life had recently passed by, and linked you and the traveler in time and place. Now with this steady track leading up the mountain and out of sight, I couldn't help but imagine that the giant carnivore might be just over the ridge and coming back this way with some of its friends.

There was something deliberate about the tracks. The dinosaur was intent on a certain direction. Did it see something? Was it after food?

The local story was that there had been an earthquake in the 1960's that had triggered a landslide. The rock and earth must have slid off the smooth shale surface like someone up-ending a fully set Thanksgiving table. On a rainy day like ours, it was clear the elements would eventually erase the great tracks.

Lockley even estimated that had the giant been active for an hour a day it would have covered more than 12 miles. He played this out to its logical end: Twenty-six animals could accumulate more than 60 miles a day by being active for one hour a day, covering 400 miles week or about 1,750 per month. A relay of two dozen dinosaurs, Lockley observed, could have walked the entire length of the Silk Road from Venice to Beijing in less than four months. His reference to the Silk Road conjured an image of Marco Polo and his uncles traveling by dinosaur instead of camel.

I had wanted to leave a mark on the land I had explored for nearly two years. Now here we were before marks that had been left over 150 million years ago. This changed things. These creatures were giants and what had they left? Footprints. In the right place at the right time and through a rare combination of the elements, their tracks had been preserved for more than 2 million of my lifetimes. The footprints illustrated the answer to my question—what was the point of trying to leave a mark? Was it just so someone could look at it 100 or 200 years later?

Monuments were being built all over the country to honor its leader. How long would they last? They were only physical symbols of a man.

I altered my goal and decided not to leave a physical mark but something distinctly human. It would be to leave some positive influence, however slight, on at least one person in Turkmenistan. This did not come from a feeling of superiority; it was from being an outsider. Travelers have always had the power to stimulate a culture with outside knowledge. The travelers of the Silk Road influenced each other by exchanging ideas. Marco Polo stimulated Ghengis Khan's curiosity about Europe—enough to want to conquer it, perhaps. Sailors in the port of Liverpool influenced modern music when the Elvis records they carried in their sea bags were bought and played by local high school students like John Lennon and Paul McCartney.

* * *

The next month I sold my Jeep to a Turkmen friend and left Turkmenistan. My last night on the compound, I parked the Jeep in its usual space under the carport. I gave it a friendly pat on the hood and a short blessing. It was near midnight when an Embassy car came to take me to the airport. I looked to back to where the Kopet Dag were hidden in the darkness. They had served as stony sentinels for two years.

I left Turkmenistan the same way I came in—in the middle of the night under the fluorescent lights of the CIP lounge. I was retracing my steps to board a 2:00 a.m. Lufthansa flight to Baku. The lounge was an antiseptic space that had always felt more like a science fiction setting, as if I was entering a transporter room for space and time travel. I replayed the images of the second day when I saw the bearded man on the motorcycle with a sidecar.

I walked the tarmac to the waiting Airbus awash in two years of images and thoughts. I had been thinking about Eileen and Charlotte since they left over seven months ago; but I also thought about the dedicated and hopeful Turkmen I had met. I may have put a greater premium on friendships in Turkmenistan than at home because I was an outsider in a controlled society. By talking to an American, especially one associated with the Embassy, my friends risked questions or harassment from the secret police. This made their loyalty and kindness count for more than usual. In the face of all these challenges, Guljahan, Serdar, Dovelet and his family, and others were willing to introduce Eileen and me to their culture.

I wondered where Turkmen got hope. People like Dovelet had to struggle to provide a future for his family in a place where he needed permission to do everything. When I met young people in schools, I realized they had almost no educational or professional opportunities unless they could find the money to buy them. I wondered how many of them could find the enthusiasm for the future. They seemed full of hope to study abroad. In the back of my mind I thought how the simplest thing like entering college or traveling from one city to the next either proved to be extremely difficult or out of the question for the average Turkmen. Some observers predicted the worst features of the Turkmenistan's regime would intensify: more purges, greater religious persecution, and even more isolation from the outside world. I doubted I would have the same patience and optimism as Dovelet—but then again, what choice did he have?

* * *

I knew I was back in the West when the German Lufthansa flight attendant told me in a British accent to fasten my seat belt.

There is always certain sadness at the end of something. I would miss Turkmenistan. It was a world unknown to me. It was truly a lifetime experience, expanding and changing my views like a two-year *Outward Bound* course. It was likely to be the most challenging place I would ever work. I had the autonomy to manage an office, for a time, as the sole American. At the same time, I was going home feeling I was making a fresh start, as if I was leaving college. I had turned forty during my time in Turkmenistan. Being there felt like a positive beginning to life and that I could learn something completely new.

I had a comfortable job and life but hoped for something outside of it, something meaningful outside of myself. Turkmenistan had been an world outside of my awareness. I had explored a blank space on the map but unlike Conrad's Marlow, I had been able to return without "the horror." I saw a world operating outside myself. I stepped into it for a time as an observer. The same people operated in that world as before I came there. Their lives and jobs would go on as before. I was out of their consciousness, in it for a time, and then left the country to fade away.

When the male Lufthansa flight attendant offered me a tray of European style baguettes, I asked if I could take two. In the subtlest mocking tone he responded, "Would you like a drink with your meals?"

Sometimes you do not know what you want. I knew I wanted two baguettes but two years ago I did not think that I wanted to live in Turkmenistan. I found that I liked living here. This was one of life's great surprises. But right now I wanted to be back in the West.

When I came home to northern Virginia, I was not sure whether I had any influence on even one Turkmen. Turkmenistan influenced me, however. Our family adopted the Turkmen custom of removing our shoes at the door. Each time I slipped them off and piled them together with Eileen and Charlotte's, I remembered the pile of shoes in the *Archena's* home and the tracks of the giants of Khodja Pil Ata.

This was the end of my Turkmen adventure.

— END —

ACKNOWLEDGEMENTS

When you are a guest in a country where you do not speak the language, understand the culture, or know what not to eat, you are especially indebted to its people who offer friendship and hospitality. Our Turkmen friends acted as guides, interpreters, and teachers. They opened their homes to my family and shared their meals, histories, and personal stories. My journeys around Turkmenistan would not have been possible without them. Much as they deserve credit here, I have changed their names, and sometimes characteristics, to protect their privacy.

The raw material for this book came from my personal journals. Special thanks to Greg Lastowka, the creator and webmaster of www.Chaihanna.com who agreed to post some of my material. Thanks to Ambassador Stephen Mann and Ambassador Laura Kennedy and Country Director Murl Baker who encouraged me to keep writing. Thanks to the members of Embassy Ashgabat and USAID offices in Ashgabat and Almaty. Also thanks to Scott Yeutter who helped arrange guides for the trip to Devkesan. In some cases, identities of Embassy colleagues have been changed for their personal privacy.

Thanks to Jamie Stiehm and Michael Gray of the *Baltimore Sun* who published excerpts of Journey 3. Trevor Aaronson and James Plouf of *Marco Polo Magazine* who featured an excerpt from Journey 5. Thanks also to David Jones of *The Washington Times* and Steve Honley of the *Foreign Service Journal*. I am also indebted to Lyn Boone and Paul Pegher of Denison University and Cathy Cossman of Radio Free Europe/Radio Liberty.

Thanks to Cathy Rojko, Sara Prosser, Violonda Botet, Bruce

Weinrod, Jim Slaugh, Susan Roberts, the late Paul Estaver, and the Warrenton Writers Group who provided advice and allowed me to inflict upon them various drafts. Also, I'm indebted to Tim Wells, Daniel Hays, and Peter Hessler. Special thanks to Tom Bissell who offered kind words of encouragement and suggested the title. I owe a special debt to Kathryn Sultzbaugh who encouraged me to write a book and then offered constant advice and support.

To my father, Walter, who served as my Turkmenistan news clipping service, and to my mother, Mary; parents-in-law Hank and Aggie Lewison; and to Charlie and Patricia Kropf both of whom always offered us a second home whenever we needed it.

Last, for my wife Eileen and daughter Charlotte, who lived through the experience the first time and then put up with it a second time during weekends and evenings when I took to writing *Unknown Sands*. It is to them that this book is dedicated.

EPILOGUE

"[Turkmenistan] is the kind of place that can show up on the front page in a few years and take everyone by surprise."
-- Theodore Karasik, RAND Corporation

In some ways returning can be harder than departing. Call it reverse culture shock. I had to readjust to the accelerated pace of life in the U.S. and return to my job as an attorney at State Department Headquarters. It was difficult to step back and give up the autonomy that I had exercised under an extraordinary time. Over the next year our family regrouped and worked to fit back into life in Northern Virginia. We bought a house and I took up fighting Washington area traffic. Eileen resigned her commission for the more important task of raising our daughter.

Contact with Turkmen friends was difficult at best. I knew all our emails would be read by the Turkmen authorities. I scanned the newspapers for scraps of information on Turkmenistan. Most stories were "fly-by" comic accounts focused on the presidential cult of personality and Niyazov's bizarre edicts. *The New York Times Magazine* featured a story on Turkmenistan entitled "When a Kleptocratic, Megalomaniacal Dictator Goes Bad." Some commentators have issued more alarmist predictions by what they see. The London- based International Crisis Group said, "There's a real risk that it could become the next Afghanistan, and it could certainly become a danger to the rest of the world." The *Economist* even voted Turkmenistan to be the world's worst place to live in 2004.

By contrast, my own impressions had less to do with the Turkmen President for life and more with the impressive character of the Turkmen people. They are very proud and given the chance to live abroad or remain in their homeland would remain. Despite the fact they live under a government that has changed little from Soviet times, I understand their desire to remain in the land of their birth and heritage. It is their homeland where they were born and raised and their families live. They are patient and seem to be waiting for a time when things might improve and they can be a part of it. What was most remarkable is that the Turkmen demonstrated their hospitality under the most difficult circumstances when the KNB (Turkmenistan's secret police) closely monitored their communications and contacts with foreigners.

President Niyazov continues to build monuments including one to his book the *Ruhnama* as well as central Asia's largest Mosque that he located in his hometown. He was also the target of an assassination attempt, in which the exact facts of who did what to whom are still unclear, followed by a series of show trials. Most ominously, he is curtailing the education system by having reduced the number of years of high school education, prevented students from studying abroad and invalidating all degrees earned outside of Turkmenistan. For that reason my greatest sympathy is with the Turkmen people.

Personally, the full effect of my two years has given me a better appreciation of Turkmenistan while at the same time a better appreciation of my own country. For me, travel makes the best stories. Look at the second major book of Western Civilization and it is *The Odyssey*.

That's the end of the story but secretly I'm waiting for that next journey.

SELECTED BIBLIOGRAPHY

Allworth, Edward, ed. *Central Asia; A Century of Russian Rule.* New York: Columbia University Press, 1967.

Barthold, V.V., (V. and T. Minorsky, trans). *Fourt Studies on the History of Central Asia.* Leiden, Netherlands: E.J. Brill, 1962.

Blunt, Wilford. *The Golden Road to Samarkand.* New York: Viking Press 1973.

Christian, David. *A History of Russia, Central Asia, and Mongolia: Inner Eurasia from Prehistory to the Mongol Empire.* Malden: Blackwell Publishing, 1998.

Curtis, William Eleroy. *Turkestan: The Heart of Asia.* New York: Hodder & Stoughton, George H. Doran Company 1911.

Foltz, Richard C. *Religions of the Silk Road: Overland Trade and Cultural Exchange from Antiquity to the Fifteenth Century.* New York: St. Martin's Press, 1999.

Gibb, H.A.R., *The Travels of Ibn Battuta, Vols. I, II, III.* London: Hakluyt Society, Syndics of the Cambridge University Press, 1956.

Grousset, Rene. *The Empire of the Steppes a History of Central America.*

Rutgers, NJ: Rutgers University Press, 1970.

Hays, Jr., Otis. *Home from Siberia : The Secret Odysseys of Interned American Airmen in World War II.* College Station, TX: Texas A&M University Press, 1990.

Holt, P.M., ed. *The Cambridge History of Islam.* Cambridge Press: Cambridge U.K. 1970.

Hopkirk, Peter. *The Great Game: The Struggle for Empire in Central Asia.* New York: Kodansha International, 1992.

Hopkirk, Kathleen. *A Traveller's Companion to Central Asia.* London: John Murray, 1993.

Curtis, Glenn E., ed. *Kazakstan, Kyrgyzstan, Tajikistan, Turkmenistan, and Uzbekistan: Country Studies*, Federal Research Division, Library of Congress: Washington, D.C. , U.S. G.P.O., 1997.

Krader, Lawrence. *Peoples of Central Asia*. Uralic and Altaic Series, No. 26. Bloomington: Indiana University, 1963.

Lamb, Harold. *The March of the Barbarians*. New York: Doubleday, Doran & Company, Inc., 1941.

Lansdell, Henry. *Russian Central Asia*. New York: Arno Press, 1970.

Lipsisu, Fank. *Alexander the Great*. New York, Saturday Review Press, 1974.

Lockley, M.G. *The Eternal Trail: A Tracker Looks at Evolution*. Reading, MA: Perseus Books, 1999.

Loges, Werner. *Turkmen Tribal Rugs*. London: Allen & Unwin, 1980. Notes: Translated from Russian by Raoul Tschebull.

Mailart, Ella. *Turkestan solo; One Woman's Expedition from the Tien Shan to the Kizil Kum*. New York: G. P. Putnam's Sons 1935. Notes: Translated by John Rodker.

Maclean, Fitzroy. *Eastern Approaches*. New York: Atheneum, 1984.

Maclean, Fitzroy. *A Person from England, and Other Travelers*. New York: Harper, 1958.

Maslow, Jonathan. *Sacred Horses: The Memoirs of a Turkmen Cowboy*. New York: Random House, 1994.

Mayhew, Bradley; Plunkett, Richard; Richmond, Simon. *Lonely Planet Central Asia (2nd ed.)*. Oakland, CA: Lonely Planet Publications, 2000.

Meakin, Annette M.B. *In Russian Turkestan: A Garden of Asia and its People*. London: G. Allen, 1903.

Marvin, Charles. *The Eye-Witnesses' Account of the Disastrous Russian Campaign Against the Akhal Tekke Turcomans*. London: W.H. Allen & Co., 1880.

Moore, Benjamin Burges. *From Moscow to the Persian Gulf, Being the Journal of a Disenchanted Traveller in Turkestan and Persia*. New York: London, G. P. Putnam's Sons, 1915.

O'Bannon, George. *The Turkoman Carpet*. London: Duckworth & Co., 1974.

Polo, Marco. *The Travels of Marco Polo.* New York: Modern Library, 2001. Notes: Edited and revised from William Marsden's translation, by Manuel Komroff; introduction by Jason Goodwin.

Rashid, Ahmed. *The Resurgence of Central Asia: Islam or Nationalism?* Atlantic Highlands, New Jersey: Zed Books, 1994.

Renault, Mary. *The Nature of Alexander.* New York: Knopf Publishing Group, 1976.

Thubron, Colin. *The Lost Heart of Asia.* New York: Harper Collins Publishers, 1994.

Shoemaker, Michael Myers. *The Heart of the Orient; Saunterings through Georgia, Armenia, Persia, Turkomania, and Turkestan, to the Vale of Paradise.* New York: G. P. Putnam's Sons, 1904.

Skosyrev, Petr, (trans. D. Skvirsky). *Soviet Turkmenistan.* Moscow: Foreign Languges Publishing House 1956.

Tyson, David. *Shrine Pilgrimage in Turkmenistan as a Means to Understand Islam Among the Turkmen.* Central Asia Monitor, No.1, 1997.

Wheeler, Geoffrey. *The Peoples of Soviet Central Asia.* Chester Springs, PA: Dufour Editions 1966.

Whitnell, Giles. *Central Asia: The Practical Handbook.* London: Cadogan Books, 1993.